PRAISE FOR DANNY SEO

This is a wonderful book,
chock full of innovative ideas, tips and solutions
to make changing the world a lot easier.
— Dr. Jane Goodall —

Danny Seo is a staunch believer
that when things need changing,
you change them.
— People Magazine —

Danny Seo's message is that of service.
By following the teachings of this activist
and entrepreneur of altruism,
you may come to find hope and purpose
for your own life, for your family, and for the world.
Danny's message is simple:
"Believe You Can, Now Do It."
— Terry Cummings, Former NBA Player —

If everything goes to plan,
Danny Seo aims to be the impresario
of a whole new lifestyle, spiritual yet stylish,
in which his followers wear hip, eco-friendly shoes
and donate their frequent flier miles
to charities for sick children.
He believes in yoking technology to philanthropy,
in pairing fashion and environmentalism,
in making activism cool.
— The Washington Post —

be the
difference

be the difference

a beginner's guide to changing the world

Danny Seo

Foreword by Deepak Chopra

NEW SOCIETY PUBLISHERS

Cataloguing in Publication Data:

A catalog record for this publication is available from the National Library of Canada.

Cover design by Diane McIntosh; photograph by Jorg Meyer.

Book and page layout by Jeremy Drought

Printed in Canada on acid-free, partially recycled (20 percent post-consumer) paper using soy-based inks by Transcontinental/Best Book Manufacturers.

New Society Publishers acknowledges the support of the Government of Canada through the Book Publishing Industry Development Program (BPIDP) for our publishing activities, and the assistance of the Province of British Columbia through the British Columbia Arts Council.

BRITISH
COLUMBIA
ARTS COUNCIL
Supported by the Province of British Columbia

Paperback ISBN: 0-86571-432-0

Inquiries regarding requests to reprint all or part of *Be The Difference* should be addressed to New Society Publishers at the address below.

To order directly from the publishers, please add $4.00 shipping to the price of the first copy, and $1.00 for each additional copy (plus GST in Canada). Send check or money order to:

New Society Publishers

P.O. Box 189, Gabriola Island, British Columbia V0R 1X0, Canada

New Society Publishers aims to publish books for fundamental social change through nonviolent action. We focus especially on sustainable living, progressive leadership, and educational and parenting resources. Our full list of books can be browsed on the worldwide web at: www.newsociety.com

NEW SOCIETY PUBLISHERS
www.newsociety.com

for Carol Holub

for keeping the spirit alive

Table of Contents

acknowledgments

WITH the publication of this new book, inspired by my first book *Generation React*, I'm reminded how much has changed since the first one hit bookstores in 1997. At that time, I thought teenagers would pick it up and use it to change the world.

And I was right. But to my delight, people of all ages were also reading it − mothers, grandparents, kids − catching on to the easy, everyday approach I used in this practical tome on community service.

With that in mind, I wanted to write *Be the Difference* to bring my version of service up-to-date. I wanted the book to reflect how people are volunteering today − and to add loads of new, helpful tips so we can continue to make our communities healthier places to live in. Even more importantly, I wanted to express how the process of giving back to the community can actually be a form of personal growth. I've learned that the more I give, the better I feel, and the more I'm able to open my heart to accept the spiritual rewards of service.

With a project like this, there are lots of people I'd like to thank.

First, special thanks to my new friends at New Society, in particular Heather Wardle for her careful editing skills and Chris Plant for his hard work pulling loose ends together.

Continued thanks to my team: Tom Carr, Angela Cheng, Jodi Peikoff, and Joe Regal. I don't know what I'd do without this hardworking group of brilliant team players who help make my dreams a reality.

Special thanks to Jorg Meyer, the young photographer who took the photo for the book's jacket.

All of my new friends at MyPotential, Inc. I look forward to a lifetime's worth of creativity with you, making content that inspires others. I am honored to be part of such a dynamic organization. A special thanks to Lizzy Shaw for introducing me to MyPotential.

Thanks to Deepak Chopra for providing such an inspiring and wonderful foreword to this book. And to Dr. Jane Goodall for her continued support of my work.

And finally, thank you to everyone who continues to find some time in their busy lives to help people in need, to improve their community, or to speak up on a cause they feel passionate about. I've always believed as long as we each do something, we can all be the difference that makes the difference.

foreword

N the great eastern wisdom traditions, there is a concept called Dharma. An individual's Dharma is their unique relationships with the ecosystem through their unique talents. When a person is in Dharma, they experience bliss and they achieve their goals through the support of nature. If you want to know what your Dharma is, close your eyes and ask yourself the following questions:

1) *If I had all the money in the world and all the time in the world, what would I do with my life?*

2) *How would I express my unique talents, and how would I use them to serve my fellow human beings and also the larger web of life?*

If you can answer those questions and put your insights into practice, you will experience the fulfillment of every dream that you've ever had and you will experience a timeless reality — because one of the other symptoms of being in Dharma is that you're having such a good time that you lose track of time!

Danny Seo's life is an expression of what being in Dharma is all about. His extraordinary success at such a young age and the creativity and energy that pour out from him are testimony to the fact that he understands, at the level of his soul, who he is, what he wants, and what his purpose in life is.

The perennial philosophies of humanity remind us that we are inseparably interconnected with the patterns of life and intelligence that weave the web of existence. What we call the environment is really our extended body – the trees are our lungs, the earth is our body, the rivers and waters are our circulation and all sentient beings are aspects of our own spirit. In the tradition of Buddhism, it is said that we are inter-beings in the inter-isness. The Rig Veda, a spiritual text from 6,000 years ago, claims that the universe is an infinite web. The horizontal strands of the web are in space. The vertical strands are in time. At each intersection of the horizontal and vertical strands is an individual. Each individual is like a crystal bead and every crystal bead reflects the light of all the other crystal beads but also the light of the whole universe.

If you read Danny's book, *Be The Difference*, you will discover how this extraordinary young man has tapped intuitively into some of the most profound insights about our role in the universe and how he has, through his own creativity, managed to use his insights to develop practical strategies that will change the world in a meaningful way.

We and the world are one. If we want to change the world, we must change ourselves. However, this principle works in the reverse as well. If the world is in trouble and out of balance, then we are also in trouble and out of balance. Please read this book carefully and put what you learn into practice. There is great wisdom here and it comes from a fresh, youthful, and enthusiastic mind. Put the principles into practice. You will change and so will the world.

Deepak Chopra, M.D.

introduction

HAVE you ever watched a story about human suffering on the TV news and wanted to do something about it? Or read a newspaper article about urban blight and immediately felt compelled to grab some trash bags and clean it up? You're not alone, but sometimes you wonder: it often feels like you are.

What can you do? Well, despite the bleak news, there is a glimmer of hope. Take yourself, for example. You picked up this book because you know what's happening to the world and you want to do something about it. Perhaps you've given money to charity, worn a pin declaring "Save the Earth!" or taken part in a charity walk-a-thon. But even though these actions are helpful, you wonder, can I do something more than a random act of kindness? Can I really use my time, energy, and talents effectively to help someone in need or make my community a better place to live? You can.

On my twelfth birthday I formed an organization called Earth 2000 with a few neighborhood kids who had the same desire I did to improve the environment and help animals. We began with small projects like aluminum can recycling and tree plantings. But a year later, I found I yearned to do more. So over the course of seven years, I expanded Earth 2000 from a three-person operation to a national organization of 25,000 teens who campaigned to save pilot whales, protected historically important forests, and empowered other teenagers to realize that they, too, had the potential to be the difference. As Earth 2000's executive director, I became a national leader in the environmental movement.

I consider Earth 2000 to be a pioneer in the youth environmental movement. So many youth-oriented groups have been heavily funded by corporations — a basic marketing technique for businesses looking to "greenwash" their image. From the start, the goal of my friends and myself was to create an organization that was led by and created for young people. It was never about posing with celebrities or winning shiny awards, but about taking a real role in the environmental movement. And our track record of successful campaigns proved that teenagers could have a real voice in this world.

Today, I'm no longer a teenager and no longer involved with the organization. But in this next chapter of my life, I still use the valuable lessons and skills I learned from running Earth 2000. I understand the power of public relations and marketing. I can look at any problem — whether it's a charity project or a day-to-day personal issue — and develop a strategic solution. I can multi-task several projects with ease and never feel overwhelmed when problems arise. These are real-life skills no classroom could've provided.

But even today, when I am running my own media company, I still receive questions from people all over the world asking me the same question: "How did you do it all at such a young age?" It was a question that always dumbfounded me. How *did* I do it all? So I sat down and looked through my notes, files and scrapbook for clues, ideas, and resources, to answer the question. And what I came up with is this book.

I remember watching a television program one evening and feeling so inspired about helping the environment that I just went ahead and did it. Perhaps it was my special talent — running a charity, the way other young people might excel in music, sports, or academics (areas that I certainly did not do well in when I was in school!). But most people don't just go "do it" — on the contrary, a lot of us probably feel overwhelmed and give up on our lofty plans to save the world.

After the publication of my second book *Heaven on Earth*, I decided to write *Be the Difference* to emphasize the personal growth aspect of giving something back to the community. Without my years of service and work, I don't think I would be the person I am today. For that reason, I'm excited to present this book to help anyone look at problems in their community and develop a concrete strategy to fix them. It doesn't matter where you live, what age you are, how much time or money you have. All that matters is that you've made the first step by picking up this book.

Suze Orman, author of the book *9 Steps to Financial Freedom*, once said that our attitude towards making money is like holding a fist under a stream of water. If that fist is tight, you can't collect any money, which is what the water represents. But if you loosen your grip, your hands open and you can begin to acccept all that you can collect. This is just like my feeling towards giving back to the community.

When you volunteer your time or speak up for a cause that you feel passionate about, for some reason you become less obsessed with earning lots of money, having a flashy car, or keeping up with the Joneses. You start placing priority on real issues. But here's the funny thing: I discovered that the more I give, the more I seem to get in return, both financially and personally. I've loosened my grip: I'm no longer placing importance on unimportant things. When I focus less on desiring "stuff," I free my mind to concentrate on real goals, instead of stressing out over how to pay for that designer wardrobe.

For that reason, I offer this book as a means of helping others to identify problems in their community and to develop concrete strategies to fix them. You don't have to give up everything in life to be a change agent. On the contrary, when you give back to the community, everything pulls together and your life, all of a sudden, seems to be on the right track.

I wrote this book not to discuss what's wrong with the world. We all know what's going on. Instead, I wanted to make it as utterly practical as possible. You will learn my secret fund-raising tips. You will master the real way to get publicity. You'll develop plans for marketing and cause-related campaigns with local businesses so you can make a difference on a dime. You'll find ways to work with local schools so young people are taught lessons in service and altruism. In addition, I share some "must know" skills that I have developed and depend on for success with my campaigns. I've also included in each chapter my thoughts about my favorite Earth 2000 campaigns to give you insight into my life.

I have learned, after launching dozens of campaigns and speaking to thousands of people, that if all of us begin taking action, we can change the world. And it is possible to work with the business community, with citizens, with children — all of us working together to eradicate problems facing our communities. I've had first-hand experience as an entrepreneur of altruism and as a businessperson in understanding how the two worlds work. And it's this symbiosis that is the foundation of *Be the Difference*.

When you open your hearts and realize how much potential you have to make a real difference, your whole perspective on the world will change. I promise it. I've devoted my life to showing people how to overcome their aversion to acts of service by demonstrating how easy and fulfilling the experience can be. That's why I trust this book will help you in your own metamorphosis from worrier to warrior.

1

the foundation:

Getting Started

*"If we don't change direction soon,
we'll end up where we're going."*

Professor Irwin Corey

I F you're like a lot of people, you'd like to contribute something positive to society. Perhaps you'd like to revive a neighborhood park, help homeless cats and dogs, or fight drug abuse in your community. But somehow, even though you know you should be more active in helping to solve these problems, you never get around to doing anything: it seems like too much work. And it seems people all around you, of all ages, are apathetic about helping, too.

The reality is more and more people are volunteering. In Canada, almost one in three (31.4%) Canadians age 15 and over volunteered for a charitable cause between 1996–1997, according to the National Survey of Giving, Volunteering, and Participating. **In total, they volunteered more than 1.11 billion hours. In the United States, an estimated 109.4 million adults volunteered in 1998, representing an 18% increase over the 93 million adults who volunteered in 1995.** So you're not alone if you want to make a difference: people all over your community are taking part.

> *The key to making a difference in the world around you is to do one simple thing: Start with small, realistic, tangible goals.*

To begin, first figure out what cause you feel truly passionate about. It's easy to watch the television nightly news and feel an instant call to action after seeing a horrific story about the ozone layer. But your stomach grumbles and dinner soon takes priority. Instead of being swayed by the press, take a moment to reflect and ask yourself: What one problem in my community would I want solved? What can I do to fix that problem? It's okay if you can't answer the second question because you'll learn how to analyze the situation in a bit, but your answer to the first question should come up immediately.

> *Working to make a difference begins with passion. What one issue is your passion?*

When I was twelve years old, I was inspired to do something about the environment. But instead of huffing and puffing to my family and friends about the state of the rainforests, I came up with a plan. I couldn't just begin saving the environment: I had to narrow my goal to something that was more specific.

This is what I asked myself: What specific issue in this topic do I want to work on? For example, if your topic is making playgrounds safer places, perhaps your goal can be to create a monitoring committee for a particular playground in your neighborhood. That's specific. But if your goal is to make all playgrounds safe, your scope is too broad. I chose to rally young people in my community (which eventually spread to the country), to join forces and work on environmental campaigns with a youth focus. The more particular you can be about your goals, the better. Take your time and be thorough. Most important, be definitive.

Now that you've narrowed your focus to a specific goal, you're ready to get started. But before you roll up your sleeves and start to build a Habitat for Humanity home, you still have one more step to take: learning *how* to make a difference.

Ninety-nine percent of all change agents work together in organized groups — individuals working together toward a common goal. A small minority of these groups are large, national organizations boasting millions of members with big bank accounts. But most of the important work being done on behalf of "the cold, the tired, and the hungry" is handled by grassroots organizations and their volunteers. They make a big difference with their small, individual efforts to solve the bigger, pressing problems.

Getting Organized

If you're working on a small project that only involves you, creating an organization may seem like a waste of time. And if it's a small project, it just might be. But if your concerns are similar to those of even a few other individuals and you come together to work together, you are technically an organization. You may be a group of only three, but collectively, you count for more.

There are thousands of organizations throughout the world, ranging from two individuals working as a team to fix up a neighborhood park to huge, regional organizations boasting a board of directors and hundreds of volunteers dedicated to feeding the city's homeless. But even with clear differences in numbers and size, all of these groups share a common bond: they all saw the need to solve a pressing problem.

"Save the Planet by the Year 2000"

My own organization was born the night before my twelfth birthday. Unable to sleep, I was watching late night television. Flipping through the channels, I landed at the beginning of a talk show, "The Morton Downey Jr. Show." Back then, Morton Downey was a political version of "The Jerry Springer Show." So here I am watching a loud-mouthed cigarette-smoking host (who is standing in an equally scary audience) arguing with guests who cared about the environment and animals. He was opposed to them. I was intrigued.

Confrontational television makes it a point to be shocking, in-your-face, and controversial. Downey decided to ridicule these environmentally-concerned guests, telling them to "get a life" and "do something more productive." But after I witnessed eye-opening footage on the program showing forests being clear-cut, whales being killed, and landfills overflowing, I wasn't entertained any more by the host's antics. Instead, I wanted to do something to help our planet.

I declared at that moment that I would do whatever possible to make a difference. I was only eleven years old, so I didn't have a plan of action or an inkling of an idea what I should do. I just knew that I had to do something. *Anything*. And even at that age, I knew that I could be part of the solution to save those trees and whales. I decided to create a group called Earth 2000 with the mission to "save the planet by the year 2000."

The next day, I told all my friends not to give me gifts for my birthday. I didn't want a Swatch watch or a Teenage Mutant Ninja Turtle action figure. Instead, I wanted them to join Earth 2000 as pioneer members. Many were enthusiastic about my plans and were ready to plant thousands of trees, while some were joyous simply because they got to keep my birthday presents for themselves.

On that day, an organization consisting of a handful of neighborhood kids who collectively had $23.57 to spend, started working to save the planet by the year 2000. Sure, we couldn't drive or vote, but we had the three things every great group needs: dedication, enthusiasm, and tenacity. And on top of that, we were young and didn't have jobs or bills to worry about, just our growing desire to make a difference. On April 22, 1989, Earth 2000 was born.

Earth 2000 accomplished a lot despite its modest beginnings. We began by planting trees, recycling cans, and raising money to protect endangered species. But after a year of doing conventional environmental campaigns, I realized we could do a lot more as young people. And as membership and support grew, so did the scope of our work. We lobbied our elected officials, worked to pass laws, helped corporations change their policies, and inspired thousands of kids to get involved. You'll learn more about these campaigns later on in the book.

You Don't Have To Start A Group

Sometimes it's not necessary to start your own organization. In fact, with over 400,000 registered non-profit groups in the United States alone, there probably already is a group you can join and help.

I created Earth 2000 because there really weren't any environmental groups run by and for young people. Sure, there were national kids' groups working on the same issues, but they were mostly run by and funded by corporations that were only interested in seeing smiling kids posing for publicity events with their CEO. I saw a real need for a youth group and created it.

So before you start passing out fliers announcing your group, give these ideas a try:

You Don't Need to Re-invent the Wheel

- **JOIN AN EXISTING ORGANIZATION.** If you see a problem you want to solve, chances are others have seen it, too. Look around your community: is there already a group working on your issue? If there is, join and offer your time and ideas. This way, you'll be able to devote more energy to the root cause of the problem and less to constructing a new organization. It is counterproductive to have two organizations working on the same problem. There is power in numbers.

- **MAKE ALLIANCES WITH OTHERS.** If there isn't a group working directly on your issue, considering joining an organization you think might be interested in broadening its mission. For example, if your goal is to provide meals for the homeless, you could join a local vegetarian society. You could convince them to initiate a program (which you enthusiastically volunteer to coordinate) to cook meatless meals for the less fortunate. Always be on the lookout for ways to contribute to and broaden the mission of other community organizations.

- **RE-ENERGIZE AN INACTIVE GROUP.** Community groups often lose their steam when they've been around for a few years. Leadership gets burnt out, people move on, and the enthusiasm wanes. But you're full of energy and ideas — and that's exactly what they're looking for. The benefit of helping an inactive organization is that usually there is already a solid volunteer base, some existing funding, and a good track record. In other words, you're not starting from scratch, which can be a real time-saver in the short-term.

How To Recharge An Organization

Many groups ranging from campus-based to big-name national organizations, have at one time or another been given new life because new, action-oriented individuals have signed on. In my opinion, recharging a group is a good thing when done for the sake of the organization's work.

For example, when a local environmental group that was founded in the 1970s realized that their work was becoming less about conservation and more about conversation, new members took on leadership roles within the group. With fresh ideas and energy, they overhauled projects, cut waste, and brought a resurgence to the group.

Many community-based organizations are also ripe for reform. Some ideas are:

- Convince a local women's social committee, such as a gardening club, to give funds to charity instead of spending them on something frivolous.
- Persuade a local country club or golf club to organize a charity golf tournament. Funds raised could be used to benefit local cash-poor charities.
- Ask a local bicycling club to add trail conservation to its agenda.

This is where creativity and innovation are key. Sometimes the best ideas are the least obvious ones. When I was doing public relations for a forest conservation group, I realized the only way they could get

> *The task is simple: just present ideas to existing organizations and help them tailor your new project into their area of interest.*

credible, mainstream attention was to divert advertising from publications that already spoke to their core audience. Instead I contacted *Martha Stewart Living* magazine and convinced them to run public service announcements for the group. The result? People who never would've thought to support a forest group were reached as a result of the ad. Thousands of people joined.

> *Unusual or even outright strange combinations are sometimes the marriages that somehow work. Innovation doesn't happen when conventional ideas are rehashed; strange juxtapositions are the ideas that can really get people going.*

How To Start Your Own Organization

You've searched high and low in your community for a group to join and you've come up empty-handed. So you decide to start your own group.

Starting a group is easy. It only takes two elements: a leader to guide the organization and a few friends to help out when needed. Keeping it running, however, takes a lot of time and dedication. Remember, when you create an organization, you are pledging to stick through the good, the bad, and the ugly times that your organization will face. In many ways, it's like a marriage. Too many times, some of us have the attitude, "I know when to leave a sinking ship." This is poor discipline. People who are always creating new organizations are probably doing it for the notoriety and are not likely to be around when the going gets tough. Rome wasn't built in a day and you won't change the world overnight.

But there will be times when the organization will be working against the clock. If your goal is of time-sensitive nature – planning an Arbor Day activity or benefit concert – then you have to plan, execute, and complete your campaign in a timely manner. After you've succeeded in doing what you set out to do, it's fine to disband and congratulate everyone for doing a good job. This is an exception to the rule, but an option you can consider nevertheless.

Perhaps the hardest part of beginning a new organization is finding people to join it. It's even harder when you live in a rural community, where the entire population equals that of a New York City apartment complex. Whatever your geographical location, you can use the following tactics to attractive prospective members.

Send Out a News Release

A news release is an announcement to the press — radio, TV, newspapers and even dot-coms — of events and happenings. Send out a release to the local press (don't bother with *Oprah* or *USA Today* unless your group is starting nationally with some major funding) and get the word out there. Be sure to include an explanation of how individuals can join your group.

In larger cities like New York and Washington, DC, your news release will have to be a real eye-catcher, since it will be only one of many. Consider using attention-getting headlines like "New Community-Service Group to Attack Root of New York's Poverty." Be creative. Get celebrity support. The media in smaller communities have fewer stories fighting for space and are more likely to run your news release as written. Also, small-town newspapers are always hungry for news; your brand-new organization may end up as a feature article instead of a blurb.

You can also hire a news wire service company to send out releases to specific metropolitan areas. This is great if your organization or project is locally centered. Your release will be sent over the wire only to journalists covering certain geographic areas — New York City, Minneapolis, or Pittsburgh, for example. And the service isn't very expensive: it's a real time-saver and can actually be more effective than mail and faxes. PR Newswire is one organization that offers this service; learn more at **www.prnewswire.com**.

Attend Community Events

Find out what special events and festivals are happening in your community and set up an information booth at as many of them as possible. (If there is a fee to set up a stand, think twice about attending; you can't waste valuable funds on exhibition fees). Distribute fliers about your group that contain the following information: the group's mission, a contact phone number and/or address, and a contact name for prospective members. Also, have a sign-up sheet so people can join right away.

> *To track the effectiveness of your media campaign for new members, assign a "department code" to your mailing address.*
>
> *For example, when an article about Earth 2000 appeared in React magazine, our address read:*
>
> *Earth 2000,*
> *P.O. Box 24, Dept. R, Shillington, PA 19607.*
>
> *We could tell how many React readers became new members by counting the number of "Dept. R" inquiries we received.*
>
> *Be sure to share the results of your department code tracking with the media that participated; they'll not only appreciate the data, but will remember you down the road for future articles. It's a smart way to develop good relations with the press.*

Post Signs

Make hundreds of photo-copies of a sign about your newly created organization. Be sure to include a phone number and/or address. Post signs in high-traffic places like coffeehouses, super-markets, and community and school bulletin boards.

Campus Media

Advertise your group in local college and high school announcements, television programs, or newspaper. It's often very inexpensive to run full-page ads. Look for available media outlets and saturate them.

Putting Your Group Into First Gear

After signing up a handful of people, the first order of business should be to find a place to meet. I do not recommend using somebody's home; it may seem ideal at first, maybe even fun, but the burden of hosting people week-in and week-out will overwhelm the host. And as the group grows, space will become a real problem. Having one, permanent, centrally-located spot makes it easier for new members to visit — you don't have to keep reminding people where the new meeting place is, and it makes little things like parking a non-issue. Consider the following options:

Colleges

- Contact the public relations office of your nearby college and ask to use a classroom for meetings. Most colleges offer rooms to local organizations free of charge. A college is an ideal location: ample parking and on-site resources like rest rooms and eating facilities make it convenient for everyone.

Corporate Headquarters

- Many corporations have conference rooms available. Contact the public relations office of a nearby corporation and ask about their policy of sharing meeting rooms with community organizations. If a member is employed by that corporation, your chances of receiving a room greatly improve.

Offices of Other Non-Profit Groups

- Ask like-minded organizations (e.g. church, animal shelter) if you can borrow their office space during non-office hours. Contact the head person to inquire about using their facilities.

"I'd Like To Bring This Meeting To Order"

Once you've booked a room and signed up a handful of enthusiastic members, your next important step is to build the group's basic structure.

> *Never, ever, pay money to use a room. If a college, corporation, or non-profit group demands monetary compensation, turn them down. No community service organization should have to pay for meeting space. It is simply not worth it.*

Every organization, whether it's a religious-based organization or political group, needs a basic structure through which a community of people can meet together and come to decisions about action. There are probably as many different ways of making decisions as there are groups of people making them. Before deciding on the structure that would work best for your group, it's wise to think about the following questions: how leadership is shared, the level of commitment expected from individuals, and the organization's level of tolerance for divergent ideas.

A few questions to consider:

1. What level of participation should people give?

2. How should news and information be shared?

3. How should new ideas be brought up?

4. How much time and energy should be spent on creating an open dialogue?

These questions help create a generic structure; it works for most new groups. At your first meeting, use the following questions to establish your "structure."

What is the mission?

The first task is to develop a clear and succinct mission statement that states simply what your whole purpose is. It should just be a sentence or two. Because you are the founder of the organization, you will likely lead the charge in establishing the mission of the group. So this is not a question you want to leave wide open; instead, ask your membership to consider the mission statement that you have prepared ahead of time. It can, and should, be tweaked and rephrased a bit, but having a general mission prepared ahead of time lets everyone knows the group's goal up front, and anyone who disagrees can leave the group at the beginning.

Who will lead the group?

There are many ways you can organize your decision-making structure; your goal is to encourage full-participation from everyone while avoiding chaos. I recommend Robert's Rules of Order with which lots of us are familiar. This advantage of this method is that it allows core members to vote on decisions and motions quickly and efficiently. As the founder of Earth 2000, I felt that it was critical that I be the group's president, helping to guide and nurture the group into a successful organization.

Elect the officials at the first or second meeting. Accept nominations for vice president (this should be a person who already understands the group's mission; a close friend is a good nominee), treasurer (someone who is honest, trustworthy, and good with money), and a secretary (a job that involves taking notes during meetings, keeping records, and writing letters).

Nominees should give a one-minute presentation as to why they are the best person for the job. Have a quick election and congratulate the winners.

How will your group make decisions?

I think a majority vote is the best way for an organization to make decisions. For example, if President Melissa Hicks wants to launch a clothing drive for the homeless, she should make a short presentation about the project at the regular meeting. If more than half the members support the project, it wins. If not, it loses. Most people like this approach.

How much funding do you need?

This is a tough question. Since you don't have a crystal ball or psychic powers, you need a general estimate as to how much you'll need. In the first year, I suggest you just aim to raise as much money as you can and base your budget based on that ever-changing figure. You can also use the skills in Chapter 2 to raise some quick funds.

When and how often will the group meet?

I put this question later for a reason: you now have a feel for how much discussion is productive. It's very helpful to have pre-set times and agendas for meetings: that way people know what to expect. It's a tough call to figure out how long the meetings should last, but try your best to keep the meetings short enough for busy folks and long enough for those who love to talk. Regular meetings are important, but don't overdo it; you'll risk overwhelming people. Having a meeting once a month is ideal; you can develop campaigns, discuss funding strategies, and update new members all at once. Plus, most people can commit to a monthly meeting. To keep people reminded of what's going on in between meetings, e-mail is the best way to go. Always avoid having meetings on Mondays and Fridays – people will forget.

Your regular meeting should have a regular facilitator. That person will likely be you, so it's a good idea to have an agenda or a rough outline of what needs to be discussed and why.

> *When e-mailing membership, include links from advertisers in the message.* Be sure to include *in your e-mail that every click raises money for your group.* You can set up an account *for free at LinkShare (www.linkshare.com) and start earning money today.*

What's your first project?

It depends. If your organization has a very specific mission – for example, starting a recycling center in your school district – you've narrowed down your choices for the first project. But if you're like most new organizations, your goal is to tackle a worldwide problem like human rights, hunger, or the environment. If this is the case, let members submit their project ideas and use the next meeting to discuss them. Use majority rule to determine which project prevails.

What's the group's official name?

Your group needs a name that is catchy, easily understandable, and liked by the group's members. People become attached to a name, so be sure to pick the perfect name in the beginning. Avoid using acronyms (e.g., Students Working Against Poverty, or SWAP); I think its overdone by too many grassroots groups. Try to use catchy, short names. If you disagree on a name and can't think of one, don't worry; your work and actions should be your top priority. A name will come.

Taking Baby Steps

You've got your members, you've got your basic structure, and you've got your regular meeting place. So, I bet you're thinking to yourself: Now what?!?

No successful group begins as a powerhouse organization; most begin with small projects, like collecting cans of food for a soup kitchen or distributing drug awareness fliers in the community. But if every new organization starts doing small projects, why do some stay small while others become big and powerful, like the Humane Society of the United States? Simple: Some groups are happy doing tiny projects and therefore remain small; others launch larger projects and develop a broader base.

Bigger doesn't always mean better. Large groups do take on substantial campaigns, achieve significant changes, and can be a very influential voice. But change at the community level can often be won by local individuals, rather than an outside force charging in. There's no right or wrong in this situation; it's just a matter of understanding the differences between big national groups and smaller community organizations.

No matter what size your group is, you can still benefit from these five tips on becoming an advocacy force.

Five Tips on Becoming an Advocacy Force

• **KEEP IT SIMPLE**. If you're having trouble finding competent people to fill positions in your group, try the one-leader approach. Despite what may be politically correct, I believe a truly successful organization starts with a leader who handles 80 to 90 percent of the work in the first year. A new organization must fulfill all of its obligations — fund raising, campaign work, and outreach activities — completely. If the work is delegated among several individuals, chances are something will not be done properly. The leader should be responsible for deciding how funds will be spent, when volunteers should meet, and what projects the organization will pursue in the first year. He or she should also lead the regular group meetings and set the agenda. After one year of one-leader ruling, the organization can begin to delegate jobs to individuals who have proven themselves competent and responsible.

- **GET REAL**. Groups that choose to pursue difficult goals (e.g., plant one million trees by the end of the year) will have a lot of disappointed members. Your first effort should be small in scale so it can be easily accomplished. For example, instead of trying to plant a million trees, make it your goal to plant ten trees over the course of one weekend. When you and your volunteers accomplish this task, everyone will feel empowered to take on larger, more impressive projects. By going after the "big project" right away, you risk making your members feel frustrated, overwhelmed, and unhappy.

- **ROME WASN'T BUILT IN A DAY**. If the thought of doing a campaign in your group's infancy sounds stressful, don't do one. Instead, create discussion groups or special events. For example, a vegetarian society might have a monthly potluck dinner. A human rights group might discuss ethics every Thursday night at the local coffeehouse. Once the momentum grows enough (and you'll know when it does), you can start to organize specific campaigns.

- **BE CONSIDERATE OF VOLUNTEERS**. A volunteer is a person who offers to help or work without reward or payment. Such people are the most important asset an organization can have and they should be treated with care and compassion. If a volunteer is unable to attend a fund-raising event or staff an outreach table, do not get angry. I'm surprised to hear story after story of volunteers who have been "fired" by an organization's president for missing an important event. You can not "fire" a volunteer. People volunteer to be part of a team effort to solve real problems – not to be yelled at and chastised. Words of appreciation for good deeds will go a long way and will earn you the loyalty you want.

• **CELEBRATE**. Take time to celebrate a successful project or campaign. For example, after your group wins a local campaign to stop the pollution of the nearby river, order pizza and have some fun at the end of the monthly meeting. Doing so will keep the group's enthusiasm and overall energy alive for future initiatives.

savetheworld.com

Whenever I lecture around the country to non-profit organizations, one of the most common questions I get asked is, "Should we have a website?" And the answer is, absolutely, positively, "Yes."

The Internet has revolutionized the way we do business, correspond with people, and even shop. And the innovations keep coming. By keeping a presence on the Internet, you keep potential members and donors informed of your work at a convenient, round-the-clock location. Building a good website doesn't take lots of money or time, but it takes a little bit of "thinking outside of the box" to get it going.

First, reserve a domain name via Network Solutions or another reliable URL address registrant company. While it may seem economical to simply put your organization on-line at a free website hosting company, your web address will be long, awkward, and hard to remember. Instead, isn't it catchier to be known as **friendsofkids.org** instead of **geocities.com/athens/ friendsofkids?** It isn't expensive to register and will be a small investment in the long term.

At some on-line domain name-registering companies, you can create a simple, good-looking website right away. They've made the process easy and, if you're a small group, this is a really good option. You can post up-to-date information on your group's mission, contact info, and upcoming volunteer opportunities. But if you want your site to do more, try this next step.

Hiring a company to build your website can cost thousands upon thousands of dollars. But with so many website design firms out there, you have an advantage that for-profit start-ups don't have: you're a charity. Like law firms that take on pro-bono cases, lots of new media companies are willing to take on projects for free. You'll get the same professional results and attention as other clients do and have a beautiful website. It's best to go on-line and do a little digging around to see who builds sites in your neck of the woods.

Whatever you decide to do, keeping an on-line presence is a necessary part of making a difference in the world. As technology makes daily life more efficient, we should use it to make our altruistic efforts easier, too. And what better way to do that than to take full advantage of what the Internet has to offer.

Growth

If your organization grows so large that it needs to hire staff members, consider becoming a 501(c) 3 corporation. In the U.S., a 501(c) 3 group is a non-profit, tax-exempt corporation recognized as such by the Internal Revenue Service. Being one has benefits:

lower bulk-mail postage rates and individual protection from lawsuits. It will also make donations tax deductible, and will encourage large foundations to consider your group for grants. It'll cost you a few hundred dollars to file with the IRS to become a 501(c) 3, but it's worth the trouble if your group plans to hire a staff. It also takes about twenty hours to prepare the application, so you may want the help of an attorney to make sure it's completed properly. If you just plan to be a local, all-volunteer organization, don't lose any sleep over it: you don't need to file.

It might a wise idea to contact a tax attorney for help in becoming a 501(c) 3 organization. The process can be confusing, it must be done with meticulous detail, and definitely can not be done overnight. And don't worry about expense: lots of lawyers will help incorporate your organization pro bono (for free), since they are required to do a certain amount of charitable work each year. Ask your members if they know a lawyer (any kind will do), and see if that person knows a good tax attorney who can help.

In Canada, organizations receive charitable status from Revenue Canada if their objectives are non-profit and their work is for the relief of poverty or the promoting of religion, education, or other activities beneficial to the community as a whole. The last definition is broad enough to include a host of organizations, including libraries and museums, animal protection groups, and recreation associations. Canadian charitable organizations pay no taxes and may issue receipts for donations that can be used by individuals to get federal and provincial tax credits. Up to 50% of an individual's net income and 50% of taxable capital gains on donations can be tax-deductible as a charitable donation. An organization called CIVICUS works to promote a worldwide community of "informed, inspired, committed citizens who are actively engaged in confronting the challenges facing humanity." Their website, **www.civicus.org**, contains information on how Canadian groups can register their group as a charitable organization.

For more information, check your local library for books about the non-profit application process. Also, there are different sets of rules and applications for becoming a registered non-profit organization in other countries. Some countries actually give taxpayer money to support issues-oriented groups. There are funds in the U.S., but unlike other countries, these are heavily restricted and difficult to obtain. Your local representative should be able to assist in guiding you in the right direction to learn how you can obtain these funds.

It's Up To You Now

Every organization, like every change agent, is different. I've provided a basic blueprint to help you lay the foundation for your new organization. It's up to you to build the mission, philosophy, energy, and projects. And with the skills and secret tips in the next chapters, you will.

If You Liked This Chapter, You'll Love:

- Just log onto **www.charitech.org** to see how corporations and citizens can work together to bring effective change to their community. Charitech works with community service groups and corporate leaders from the booming new media economy to find ways that the two can work together to make a difference in the communities they serve.

- Visit **www.dosomething.org** to see how America's young leaders are working to make a difference. Learn how to get grants for your project, too.

- *USA Weekend* magazine sponsors "Make a Difference Day," a nationwide, day-long event where people get together to improve their community. Sponsored in part by Wal-Mart, groups of people doing something to make a difference on that day are eligible for a $1,000 grant to get their project off the ground. Lots of ideas and resources on the website; visit **www.usaweekend.com**.

- Log onto **www.oprah.com**, the website for "The Oprah Winfrey Show." Oprah Winfrey is using her television show to demonstrate to her viewers how to open their hearts and see how fulfilling and meaningful acts of service can be. Click on "Oprah's Angel Network" and read inspiring stories of ordinary people who are doing extraordinary things; you might be inspired to come up with your own service project.

- Project America, founded in 1993 by three college students, works to empower individuals to make an impact on their community. Project America works with companies, large member organizations, and non-profit groups of all sizes to design projects that people of all ages can get involved with. Visit **www.project.org** to learn more.

2
fundraising 101:

Beyond Nickels and Dimes

"Lack of money is no obstacle.
Lack of an idea is an obstacle."

Ken Hakuta

PICTURE yourself at a bake sale. The temperature outside is 100 degrees; the fudge brownies have melted; three volunteers forgot to show up; and on top of that, nobody wants to buy your cakes and cookies. After spending hours of your time baking, wrapping, pricing, selling, and cleaning, you've collected a measly twenty, thirty, or — if you're really lucky — forty dollars. You think to yourself, "Is this really worth it?!?"

We've all been there. Who among us hasn't participated in a fundraiser, frittering away our free time raising a very small amount of money for charity?

Growing up, lots of my peers in school excelled in fields such as sports, academics, and music. My talent? Fund-raising. For some odd reason, I couldn't play baseball to save my life, earned a D-minus grade point average in high school, and sang as if a frog had decided to live in my throat. But raise $1,000 in one day? Not a problem.

It was an odd talent to have. But I was glad to have it and I'm even more happy to share it with you. The reality is, raising money for your favorite charity doesn't have to take a lot of time, manpower, skills, or even luck. In fact, sometimes all it takes is a five-minute phone call to get some cold, hard cash.

Don't Follow The Leader

Volunteer groups all over the country take part in what I call "typical" fund-raising events: Candy bar sales, T-shirt sales, bake sales, and car washes. In my opinion, such "solutions" take too much time, use too many volunteers, and only generate a small amount of money despite all the hard work.

> Never, ever, do a fundraiser that other community groups are already doing. The secret to raising significant sums of money is to coordinate events that are fresh, original and creative.

There's a common notion out there that fund-raising for community organizations has to involve hard, strenuous, multi-volunteer events that take months of planning and coordinating. Again, fund-raising doesn't have to be difficult. In my eight years of fund-raising activity, I have never stood behind a booth selling cookies, gone door to door hawking trinkets, or washed a car in the name of charity. I did, however, generate up to $2,000 a day by creating innovative fund-raising campaigns that fulfilled my three basic criteria: the project took no time to prepare, cost no money up front, and only needed one or two volunteers for completion.

I discovered these perfect fundraisers several years ago. In 1989, when I needed seed money for Earth 2000, I wasn't enthusiastic about the idea of selling candy bars to the public or begging my neighbors for their spare change. Instead, I wanted a quick, simple method that would raise thousands of dollars with very little effort. Like most novice change agents, I thought those dream fundraisers just weren't possible. Fortunately, I was wrong.

"When in Doubt, Ask"

One fundraiser I happened to stumble upon was conceived during a visit to my local shopping mall. I noticed small children and their parents throwing spare change into the water fountains for good luck. As I looked into the pools of shimmering water, I wondered, "What happens to all this spare change?"

When in doubt, I always say, ask. I asked the mall management office outright, "What happens to all those coins in the water fountain?" They assured me that they didn't profit from it, but instead gave the money to charity. The problem, they said, was that many local organizations didn't want it because heavy buckets of wet, smelly coins were too difficult to deal with. After all, who had the time to clean, dry, and hand-wrap literally thousands upon thousands of coins? Again, when in doubt, ask.

So I called the U.S. Mint and asked how I could get buckets of wet coins counted without resorting to cleaning, drying, and hand-wrapping. Seconds later, a man picked up the phone and said, "Mutilated Coin Division." They actually had a whole department in the U.S. Mint devoted to counting mutilated coins. I couldn't believe it. So with a phone call to the shopping mall, they gave me several buckets of wet coins, which I took to the closest division of the U.S. Mint; from there, the U.S. Mint wired the total amount to our checking account in the amount of $2,500. And all it took was two phone calls.

Clever, isn't it? Here are some other easy fund-raising ideas you can try:

Consign Old Clothing

You can make money by selling old clothing. Consignment shops sell used clothing the way an auto dealer sells used cars. To find the closest consignment shop, look under "Consignment" or "Thrift Shops" in the phone book. Call a local shop to set up an appointment and new account. Collect old clothing from your friends, family and volunteers. Separate the pieces according to seasons – heavy jackets and sweaters for winter, shorts and T-shirts for summer – to comply with the store's requirements. Your old clothing will be sold to customers under a fifty-fifty agreement. For example, if a used jacket sells for $10 in the store, you will receive $5 and the store will keep $5. Each store is different, so shop around for the best deal.

Recycling Clothes

The American Clothing Recycling Company is a commercial recycler, not a charity, that buys clothing and shoes that they recycle for use all over the world for less fortunate men, women, and children to wear. They pay by the pound. For example, for 5,000 pounds of clothing (which is approximately 275 garbage bags), you receive $300. This can really add up when you have an entire community cleaning out their closets during a special week-long clothing drive. Learn more at **www.americanrecycling.net** if you'd like to organize a clothing recycling drive.

Collect Scrap Metal on Spring Clean-Up Days

One person's junk is another person's fundraiser. Spring Clean-Up Days allow a community's residents to dispose of large bulky items such as furniture and major appliances. Often, valuable scrap metal – including brass bed headboards, copper wiring, and steel containers – are thrown out. With a pickup truck, you and your friends can collect this discarded metal. Your local scrap metal dealers will pay good money for these items – they make money by selling it with other scrap metals to manufacturers for recycling. Contact a local scrap metal dealer about rates and requirements for purchase.

Rebates

In Pennsylvania, the Redner's supermarket chain gives one percent rebates to local community-service groups. One percent of the total grocery receipts collected by the group is refunded in the form of a monetary donation. This program is so popular that volunteers scour the store's parking lots for discarded receipts; it has become a fund-raising fixture for many community-service organizations. Contact your local supermarket to see if they offer a similar program. If not, propose they start one.

Another chain of health-food supermarkets designates a "percentage day" at one of their stores to benefit the community in which they do business. Up to five percent of one day's total sales goes to charity; often, the organizations don't have to do anything but pick up a check at the end of the day. Thousands of dollars are raised as a result of such simple schemes. Local coffee shops, bakeries, warehouse shopping clubs, and restaurants are also good places to set up percentage days. It's good cause-related marketing for them, and it's an easy fundraiser for you.

Ask a Local Baker for Free Pies and Cakes

Instead of spending hours baking your own pies and cakes (plus having to use valuable funds to buy ingredients), ask a local baker for a donation of their excess baked goods. Most companies bake hundreds or even thousands of products every day, so a donation of a hundred pies is minimal to them. Most of the time they're glad to unload excess goods by giving them back to the community: it's good PR for them. Sell the goods the same day you receive them in a high-traffic area (people, not cars!) at a reasonable price. Be sure to get permission ahead of time to set up a booth. Every penny you earn is 100 percent profit. Unsold baked goods can be given to volunteers or to your local shelter.

Organize a Tree-Activity

This fund-raising project is a Christmas tree decorating competition between several organizations. Get permission from a local shopping mall or outlet center to set up a Christmas tree display for three weeks. Each group participating is responsible for setting up a tree (live or artificial) and decorating it in the chosen theme. Donation boxes are placed in front of each tree so shoppers can vote for their favorite with monetary donations; each dollar is one "vote." All groups keep the donations they earn. The tree that gets the most "votes" (total dollar amount) wins an extra prize of $100 courtesy of the shopping mall management office.

Sell Trees

In the U.S., the National Arbor Day Foundation has a super fund-raising program that gives your group a percentage of the total sales for every tree you sell. It's simple. You collect orders from friends and family. The foundation then ships the trees to each customer via the U.S. Postal Service and guarantees that each tree will grow or be replaced free of charge. This U.S.-only program is a one-step fundraiser any group can do. For more information, write the foundation at: **211 North 12th Street, Lincoln, NE 06508-1497**.

Check the Local Newspaper

Many community-service organizations offer mini-grants for grassroots projects. Check your newspaper's community log and television public access announcements for word of any funding grants. Many newspapers also maintain comprehensive websites that archive news bits like this; use their search engine to locate awards.

Hold a Raffle

An in-kind donation is an item donated to a charity instead of a monetary gift. Ask local businesses for in-kind goods for a raffle fundraiser. Items like portable CD players, T-shirts, and gourmet food baskets are great prizes. Local national chain stores like Best Buy and Wal-Mart usually do not give free items to groups: it's a corporate policy. Instead, ask locally based businesses. Sell tickets at one dollar apiece to friends, family, and coworkers; be sure to write their name, address, and phone number on the back of each ticket.

What About Special Events?

So, you might be asking yourself, "What about a benefit concert or dance?" These can be fantastic fundraisers if you have the manpower, volunteers, and guaranteed ticket sales to pull it off. But they can be huge money-losers if executed improperly. Public relations executives who organize special events in the name of charity often raise thousands, if not millions, of dollars but end up in the red after all the expenses are paid for. Yes, there are events that do generate lots of money for charity, but they are the exception, not the norm. Plus, these events can take months to plan — valuable time which could've been used for advocacy work.

It's up to you. If you want to do a special event, partner with a corporation and let them handle all the details. Get a guarantee as to how much your group will receive for participating and do your best to get the word out there.

Corporate Handouts

Those of you who don't mind taking a fund-raising gamble can ask local companies and wealthy non-profit groups for funding. It's different from the other methods because the results can be mixed. If you're great at pitching ideas to corporate decision makers, you could make a lot of money. If just the thought of talking to a company CEO scares you, you're much better off with my nontraditional fund-raising tips. But if you want to give it a try, here are the facts you'll need to get some corporate funds.

"Let's Do Lunch"

Many organizations hire development directors whose only job is to get major funding from corporations. They create expensive grant proposals, initiate meetings with granters, and even schmooze corporate heads with fancy dinners and gifts. This, in my opinion, is the wrong approach for the novice. After all, who enjoys schmoozing?

Corporate staffers who dispense grants receive floods of slick proposals, hear the same fast talk from development directors, and receive T-shirt after T-shirt as thank-you gifts. To the corporate head, this is mundane and predictable. Instead, let's try a different approach: let them approach you, instead of you approaching them.

Talking the Talk: A Glossary of Corporate Terms

You've got to talk the talk to get the support. Here are some terms you need to know when asking corporations for money:

Action grant:	Given to fund active programs and not research projects.
Annual report:	A yearly financial report prepared by the management of a corporation.
Beneficiary:	The recipient of the corporate gift.
Capital campaign:	A fund-raising campaign over a period of years to raise major funds for projects.
CEO:	Chief Executive Officer
Donor:	The one who makes the contribution.
Fund-raising appeal:	A presentation made to potential donors.
In-kind donation:	A donation of physical items (such as computers) or services (such as book-keeping) in place of monetary donations.
Joint funding:	A grant of funds from several sources.
Letter of Intent:	A document with which a corporation commits to a certain amount of funding.
Matching gift:	A donation given with the understanding that the beneficiary will receive an equal amount from another funding source.
Philanthropist:	A person who gives substantial amounts of money to charity.
Public charity:	A tax-exempt 501(c)3 IRS-determined organization.
Query letter:	The first letter of approach to familiarize a business with a group's mission.
Unrestricted gift:	A donation with no strings attached which the beneficiary can put to any use.

Okay, now a quick psychology lesson. Why do we give? Simple: the desire to make the world a better place is a natural human instinct. But granters feel as if they're just doing another job, not helping the planet, when they hear and see the rhetoric of professional fundraisers. All of the sudden, they aren't funding worthy causes, but giving a certain professional fundraiser a token gesture to get them off their back. Why not separate yourself from the pack by highlighting how worthy your group truly is. If they can "discover" your project, if you can excite them about your cause, they might want to rescue your project with a big, fat check.

How to Get Discovered by Hollywood

I learned this just a few years ago when I placed a half-page advertisement in the program guide of the Genesis Awards, a televised awards program honoring animal-friendly movies, television shows, and journalists. I knew big names attended the event — celebrities like Pierce Brosnan, Dennis Franz, and Alicia Silverstone, as well as major movie producers, philanthropists, and entertainment executives. For just $400, I placed an Earth 2000 advertisement in the hands of one thousand Hollywood players, many earning multimillion-dollar salaries. And because I designed the ad myself, it lacked the slick look of professional ads, which ironically made it more appealing to the audience. The advertisement forced people to read it because it looked so amateurish. The ad had the right elements for a perfect "discovery" fundraiser: a wealthy, sympathetic audience and the right, downplayed look. If just one or two of these luminaries saw the ad, I believed, they would donate a few hundred dollars to support Earth 2000, perhaps becoming regular donors down the road.

I was wrong; we raised thousands and thousands of dollars. Because I didn't assign a department code to the mailing address on the advertisement, it was impossible to know for sure how many Genesis attendees actually sent checks. But counting the returns from Hollywood and Beverly Hills alone, we raised $10,000. It was the easiest fundraiser I ever coordinated.

I've proven my theory that people enjoy "discovering" and funding new organizations. But since most of you probably don't have hundreds of dollars to advertise at big Hollywood events (though if you do have the cash, give it a try!), here are some hints to help you get discovered with very little money.

Make a Plea in Your Local Newspaper

Every business leader and executive I know reads the newspaper religiously. Use the media skills outlined in Chapter 3 to get an article about your group or project into the local paper. The headline of your news release should read something like "Local Project Seeks Corporate Funding" or "Highly Praised Project to End if No Funding Found." You want sympathy. With headlines like that, some corporation is bound to want to help you. Also, be sure to get an address printed at the end of the article to encourage smaller donations from readers.

Ask in Person

Store grand openings, social gatherings, and your neighbor's backyard barbecue are all opportunities to be discovered by corporate executives. You never know when you will meet someone important. Introduce yourself to funders by initiating the conversation with questions about or compliments on their business. This is called networking. Don't be afraid to talk about the good work you and your friends are doing; when it comes to community-service, you don't need to be modest about it. I've asked lots of powerful CEOs for money to support really good causes and lots of times they've been happy to help.

Write a Nonprofessional-Looking Letter to the Company

This doesn't mean scribbling something illegible on a scrap of paper. What it does mean is writing a personal letter sent in a hand-addressed envelope. Call the company you want to fund your organization and ask for the name of the grants/community director. Write to that person and mention in the first paragraph why you're writing; do not beat around the bush. Your letter should hook them immediately. A mother might write, "Dear Ms. Smith: When my eleven-year-old daughter came home from school last year, she asked me, 'What is marijuana?' I found out that she was offered drugs in her school, right here in our community. This led me to create a local organization to effectively combat drug abuse." Be succinct, compelling, and specific. Ask them for a specific amount of funding and tell them exactly how that would be spent.

> Think about it:
> The next time
> you receive your mail,
> which letter
> would you open first?
> An envelope with
> a computer generated label
> or one that's hand-addressed?

Funding From Non-Profits

Don't overlook asking like-minded national non-profit groups for funding. Groups like The Nature Conservancy, United Way, and the Humane Society of the United States generate hundreds of millions of dollars each year. To them, a donation of $1,000 to your group is peanuts; it represents as little as .01 percent of their total available funds. Send a letter requesting funds to either the president, chief executive officer, or executive vice president of the non-profit organization. Staff members of national organizations usually don't have the authority to dispense grants.

It is unrealistic to think you'll get funded every time you approach someone; there's a lot of competition out there for the same funds. It takes patience and determination to create the perfect marriage between a corporation and an organization. To keep you going, remember this: corporate donations and easy fundraisers beat a bake sale any day.

Where To Keep Your Funds

All of your organization's funds should be kept in a bank checking account. Specifically, you should open an account that requires a minimum balance no larger than one hundred dollars ($100). Shop around for the best deal. In Canada, some credit unions offer free services to community service organizations. With so many banks competing for your business, you should open an account with free checking. Smaller banks tend to offer better deals than large, big-name institutions. If you're not careful, you could end up paying monthly fees, anywhere from three to ten dollars a month.

It should also be a joint account. That means only two people, the president and the treasurer or vice president, have the power to sign and write checks.

Cheap Checks

Don't buy checks from the bank: they tend to be pricey. Instead, purchase your checks from an outside source. You have several choices:

- **AFFINITY CHECKS.** These specialty checks support various U.S. national organizations. You can choose which organization receives a portion of your purchase. Groups which benefit include Habitat for Humanity, World Wildlife Fund, and Stand for Children. Affinity checks aren't available in Canada yet, but at press time, several companies were promising they would "be available very soon." Contact: **Message Products** at **(800) 243•2565**; or visit their website at **www.messageproducts.com**

- **ECONOMY CHECKS.** In the U.S. you can order checks through the mail from discount check printing companies. It only costs a few dollars to print a couple of hundred checks through them. Check the Sunday newspaper coupon circular for a list of choices or contact **Current, Inc., 1005 East Woodman Road, Colorado Springs, CO 80920**, for a catalog or by e-mail: **currentcustomerservice@currentinc.com**

- **PAY ELECTRONICALLY.** Hasn't the Internet made so many time-consuming chores easier? Find out if your bank or credit union will allow for on-line banking. This way, you'll be able to pay bills, transfer funds, and check balances whenever it's convenient. You may need to download software onto your computer, but the extra hassle is sure worth it.

Invest

If you're lucky enough to have a good cash-flow, consider investing some money in a high-performing mutual fund, or at the least, keeping it in a money market account. You'll earn higher returns on your money than keeping it in an interest-bearing account at the bank, and you'll always have access to it if your organization needs the funds. Read *Get a Financial Life* by Beth Kobliner (Simon & Schuster, 2000) to learn more about the nuts and bolts of investing.

You also might want to consider investing your money in a socially-responsible fund. These mutual funds avoid companies that pollute the environment, sell tobacco, and have a track record of labor problems. You can read *Investing With Your Values: Making Money and Making a Difference*, by Hal Brill, Jack A. Brill and Cliff Feigenbaum (New Society Publishers, 2000). A good socially-responsible fund in Canada is Ethical Funds; you can reach them at **1441 Creekside Drive, 8th Floor, Vancouver, BC V6J 4S7**, Phone: **1 (877)•ETHICAL**, Fax: **(604) 714•3859**, or on-line at **www.ethicalfunds.com**

It's also a good idea to have your books managed by a certified public accountant (CPA). Again, look for a qualified CPA with good recommendations — someone who will manage your books on a pro bono basis. This way your funds will be properly managed and potential donors will feel more confident to give to your organization since the bottom line is always being watched.

- The Funding Center helps non-profit organizations worldwide with fund-raising. For a copy of their publication, *The Funding Manual: A Guide to Proposal Preparation*, contact them at: **901 King Street, Alexandria, VA 22314**.

- Your local library probably has a selection of material devoted to the art of fund-raising. There have been hundreds of books written on the subject. Peruse these books for inspiration and pick out your favorite ideas.

If You Liked This Chapter, You'll Love:

- Good money management will not only help you spend your group's funds efficiently, but it can also be used to help you in your own personal expenses. An ideal place to start is at the bookstore. *9 Steps to Financial Freedom* by Suze Orman (Crown, 1999) is a good choice.

- Keep inspired. Visit **www.fund-raising.com** for a list of resources, companies, and ideas for new and clever fundraisers.

- If your group has a website, add an on-line shopping mall to your site. Every time someone clicks through to a retailer via your website, you'll receive a percentage of the purchases they make. Check it out at **www.igive.com** — they can link up your site with on-line retailers.

3

outreach:

Getting the Word Out with PR

*"Genius is one percent inspiration
and 99 percent perspiration."*

Thomas A. Edison

It may seem like an odd thing to say, but public relations has always been an enjoyable hobby for me. I like the challenge of taking a concept, a message, or an idea and sharing it with the world. Whether it's planting story ideas in magazines, working with TV producers on segment ideas, or organizing on-line events to tie-in with a book launch, I find the process creative, fulfilling, and even a lot of fun.

Most people, I've realized, don't share this sentiment. It's tough to get attention, and the constant flow of rejection from magazine editors and TV producers can be overwhelming at times. The reason people fail to get good PR, I've come to realize, is not due to a lack of hard work or enthusiasm, but to a lack of understanding of what PR is.

Creating a public relations campaign is taking the ordinary, like a rock tied with a piece of string, and making it extraordinary by calling it a Pet Rock. The public relations industry influences our buying habits, our positions on social issues, and a myriad of our other decisions. If you've got a cause and you want to tell the world about it, you need to know how to turn your issue into a hot story that every radio, television, and print journalist will want to cover.

Martha Stewart: The Role Model

I never realized just how powerful the media could be until my best friend, Melissa Hicks, told me in 1993 to watch a show on cable television called "Martha Stewart Living." "She's really funny," Melissa said. I watched this blonde know-it-all expert teach me how to make puff pastry, go fly-fishing, and create an impromptu party on the beach for unexpected guests. I thought, "Who has ever had an impromptu party on the beach? She's funny because she's not in touch with the average person." With a little research, I soon discovered Martha headed a multimillion dollar empire consisting of books, "signature" products ranging from house paint to cookie cutters, her own magazine, and yes, her television show. She has created this world by taking what she's good at and marketing herself as the one and only person who can do it.

I didn't realize it at the time, but Martha Stewart would soon have a greater influence on me than I expected. One of the questions I'm asked most often is, "Who are your role models?" People expect me to answer with award-winning humanitarians or beloved authors, but my three role models are anything but conventional: Albert Schweitzer (okay, he's not a surprise), News Corporation chairman Rupert Murdoch, and, of course, Martha Stewart.

Albert Schweitzer taught me how to create a foundation of ethics for myself so that no matter what happens to me, I can always base my decisions on what I believe to be true. Rupert Murdoch taught me valuable business skills, showing me to take an idea, develop it into a thriving business, and protect it from outside forces. And Martha Stewart taught me this lesson: believe in yourself no matter what.

Martha Stewart gets parodied, mocked, and made fun of in the press, by her peers, and by almost anyone who has heard the name. How can anyone take pastry bags so seriously? But Martha knew she had a good idea — to create a company that makes domesticity an art form — and she wanted to be the one who was credited for creating it. So she named her TV show, books, magazine, and product line after herself. This way, she figured, no one could ever take her company away from her. Without Martha Stewart, there would be no Martha Stewart Living. So she was able to brush aside all of the jokes and mean comments, and charge ahead. And today, she's one of the most influential people in the world in the field of lifestyle — simply because she believed in herself no matter what.

After being inspired by Martha Stewart, I decided to apply some of the same principles and ideas to my own organization. As the founder of the organization, I had the passion, drive, and understanding to represent our core message. If other people could recognize me, Danny Seo, as Earth 2000, then I'd have succeeded in making our group more personable, recognizable, and identifiable.

I thought: What is going to make Earth 2000 unique? How can we gain media attention when there is a flood of other groups, causes, and news stories fighting for limited space in the media? The answer came to me: Brand myself.

So I soon became the spokesperson for the group: talking to the press, doing 4 a.m. radio programs, driving hours to tape television shows in the middle of nowhere. I figured this: At a certain point, producers and editors would begin to notice me and would soon keep my name in their Roledex under "E" for environmentalist. Anytime they were doing a story about the environment, I could be called upon for comments.

And it worked. I did thousands of interviews, and people became excited about Earth 2000. They joined by the thousands as a result of these interviews. Instead of pricey advertising, we got free promotion on TV, on radio, and in print that netted members, awareness for our campaigns, and money to fund future projects.

The lesson of this story is simple. It will be worth your time and energy to do lots of press interviews – from cable access to national TV. Becoming a spokesperson for your issue does more than bring your cause into the spotlight – it can also be a lot of fun.

So How Do I Do It?

If you want to get coverage in the press – a form of free advertising – you're going to have to learn the art of public relations. But relax. Starting a comprehensive media campaign involves just three simple steps:

- Understanding basic media terminology;
- Finding out who might be interested in your story;
- Ensuring your efforts land you in the right media outlets.

Invested properly, a few dollars spent on PR will reap an invaluable amount of media exposure.

Target One: Your Local Newspaper

A good cup of coffee and the morning paper are as American as apple pie. Watergate and Whitewater were brought to light by the print media – and taught the American public to avoid things with aquatic names. Because newspapers have the power to sway the Court of Public Opinion, they are a necessary tool for any good social campaign. By winning the support of your local newspaper, your viewpoint on the issues can reach an audience of thousands.

Newspeak: A Glossary of Terms for the Novice

- **News release**: A statement prepared specifically for the press, inviting them to cover an event or story idea. Your news release should include certain catchphrases:
    - *For immediate release*: Put this at the top of the page if it doesn't matter when the newspaper reports on your issue,
  or - *Embargo until*: Use this if your piece is "dated." For example, if you're organizing an event on March 15 and don't want it reported until after that date, write "Embargo until March 15 @ 12 a.m." on top of the page.
    - *Contact Person*: This is who the reporter should contact with questions; include a phone number (both day and night!) and an address.
    - *Date of Release*: Always include the date on a news release.
    - *Title*: Keep it simple but catchy. Avoid using articles like "the," "a," and "an." Study headlines in the newspaper for ideas.
    - End your release with "-end-" or "###."

- **Press kit**: Includes a news release, photographs, fact sheets, literature, and anything else relevant to your campaign. Some elaborate kits even include books and videotapes. Create press kits only for specific campaigns.

- **Media list**: The full names, addresses, phone and fax numbers of journalists who are sympathetic to your cause or have already reported on your past efforts.

- **City desk**: When you don't know where to send your news release, send it here. The city desk editor will forward your release to the reporter he or she thinks will be the one most interested in your story.

Writing a News Release

Writing a good news release takes a lot of time and practice, but it's worth the effort. A good release captures the attention of a reporter and can convince him or her to write a piece on your cause. Depending on the size of the newspaper, journalists receive anywhere from a dozen to a hundred news releases every week. Your challenge is to write one that sticks out from the others. A news release can generate dozens of stories or none at all. It's up to you to figure out what gets attention and what doesn't.

The first paragraph should answer the four W's: Who is organizing the event? What is the event for? When is the event going to occur? Where will it happen?

The second and third paragraphs should describe your efforts in more detail. Explain what you are doing and how you are doing it. Quote yourself or others involved. Include interesting facts relevant to your cause to make the story even more newsworthy.

Your last paragraph is like a biography. Discuss your educational background, interesting facts about yourself or the group, and other information that adds credibility.

Don't doubt yourself! If you think your news release isn't good enough (after all, you don't own a PR firm), don't worry. Many journalists enjoy (and sometimes even prefer) receiving releases from individuals and community-service groups. In the era of the information superhighway and powerhouse PR firms, many journalists like to go back to their roots and scoop a hidden story. Most of the time, your amateur effort will appeal to this need.

The Bottom Line on News Releases

• **DON'T LIE.** Like an elephant, a journalist never forgets.

• **DON'T BE AFRAID TO HYPE YOURSELF.** Though a little self-serving, it's an effective way of achieving coverage. For example, if you're a teenager, emphasize your youthfulness in the release. Ditto for senior citizens and soccer moms.

• **ALWAYS CHECK SPELLING.** Even the best PR firms have glaring errors in their news releases. The news industry is a serious business, and errors can suck away any dignity from your release. If you send-out a mistake-riddled release on the wire, have it pulled and send out the corrected version. Perfection is key.

While even the best news releases get ignored, it only takes one story to get a community motivated. Never, ever, give up.

Target Two: Other Newspaper Outlets

Today's newspapers provide multiple outlets for ordinary people to express their views on important social issues. In addition to news coverage, you can saturate the newspaper in sections designed to give the public a forum for discussion and opinion sharing.

• **Letters to the Editor.** Write a letter to the newspaper about a recently covered topic. For example, if your town decided not to fund repairs to a local playground, write a letter expressing how your kids depend on that playground for recreation and how dangerous it's becoming. Your letter will probably be published if it's well written and concise. And it only costs you the price of a stamp to voice your opinion.

- **Op-Ed Page**. This page runs editorial pieces, usually 800 −1200 words in length, on current events and controversial topics. It's written by people who give their opinion, or perspective, on a timely issue. It's difficult to get an editorial printed but worth a try if your writing skills are in pretty good shape. Read previous Op-Ed pieces to get a feel for their tone. Every newspaper wants something different.

- **Contribute**. Smaller newspapers and newsletters will gladly accept a good writer who has interesting ideas and respects deadlines. Send an editor a list of story ideas; suggest a regular column. Don't ask for money. There isn't any.

When The Silence Is Deafening

You've worked hard on your PR campaign with no results. First, study your release. Did you put the right date and time on it? Did you remember to mail it? (You'd be surprised how many people forget to do that.) Did you give ample time for the journalist to respond? Was it an abnormally busy news week? If you've answered "no" to any of these questions, then study my two most popular media "stunts" and try to incorporate them into your campaign. They've usually worked for me.

Keep Track

It's amazing how many professional PR people pitch stories to producers and editors without even knowing anything about that

TV show or publication. Watch TV, read newspapers and magazines, listen to radio programs. Become so familiar with the show that you can call a TV station and cite past segments for your pitch. "Remember that eco-friendly fashion segment you did last year? We could do something similar, but with only the best of fake fur clothing and accessories." Doing your homework goes a long way.

I booked myself on "The Oprah Winfrey Show," simply by visiting their website (**www.oprah.com**) and reading their "In the Works" page. The website indicated what topical shows were in the works and whether they were looking for guests. I simply e-mailed myself as a potential guest (which was automatically forwarded to the producer working on that segment), and got booked the very next day.

Highlight Your Highlights

Find a quality unique to yourself and focus on it in your news release. A teenager might write "Teenage Crusader Leads War on Drugs." Throughout the release, the words "youth," "young people," "teens," and "adolescents" would be used repeatedly. The point is to differentiate yourself from others by showcasing your unique quality.

Target Three: Television

Television, on a national level, is the most powerful media outlet. Oprah Winfrey, for example, reaches millions of Americans every day with her nationally syndicated talk show. Whatever book she selects for her famed book club becomes a runaway bestseller. This is power.

While your appearance on television won't cause radical changes in the stock market, you can still bring your issue to the public. But before you start your television campaign (and run to the mall for a new outfit), there are some terms you should know:

- **Talent booker**: The person responsible for booking guests on television talk shows. Not all shows have talent bookers. If the show does have one, contact him or her about being a guest.

- **Associate producer**: These people wear many hats. They're in charge of the nitty gritty involved with each show — and may be good people to contact about being a guest.

- **Supervising producer**: These people can book a guest right away. While an associate producer will want to hear your idea, they usually have to pitch it in their meetings with higher-ups in order to book you. By going through the supervising producer, you avoid that step and can get a booking on the spot.

- **Executive producer**: The boss. This is the contact person every single producer on the show reports to on the day-to-day operations of the show. They rarely book guests themselves, but will consider pitches like any other producer. The only difference here is that if they like you, your information will be transferred to another producer at the show to get booked.

Getting booked on a local television talk show is just like getting covered in your local paper. Send the talent booker or associate producer a news release, a cover letter, and a few news clippings about yourself and/or your cause. If you've done other television shows, send a list with your media kit. To find out who the booker or producer is, call the station or visit your local library and ask for a directory such as "News Media Yellow Pages," a comprehensive listing of media contacts. When composing your cover letter, make a convincing argument that your cause should be addressed on the show and that you're the person who should be addressing it. There is no room here for modesty.

How to Shine on TV

- Keep the focus on your topic and not you. Audiences don't like guests who talk about themselves.

- Watch a few shows to get a general feel for how they flow. I recommend attending a taping or two of a nationally televised talk show to get an up-close-and-personal look at how a talk show is produced.

- Don't wear clothes with confusing patterns; it looks strange on television. Instead, choose dark, solid-colored pieces. Never, ever wear a white shirt.

- Wear clean clothing. The audience has preconceived notions about grungy-looking guests. Look nice. Your mom will be so proud.

- Be sure to get an address and/or phone number superimposed on the screen so interested viewers can contact you about how they can join or help. Earth 2000 has gained thousands of members simply by appearing on a few television programs.

- Bring a blank VHS tape with you to get a copy of the show. Most television shows are willing to provide you with a copy of the broadcast. You can show the tape to prospective members and donors. Also, watch yourself at home to see how well you presented yourself on television. Learn from your mistakes.

- Never say "hi" to your friends or family. No one cares.

- Bring color photographs of your members or yourself in action. For example, bring good-quality photos of your group doing a beach cleanup: anything to make the group seem more interesting.

- Finally, have fun! If you ever watch a talk show with celebrity guests, they are at ease, personable and relaxed. Take a cue from them and have fun with your appearance on the show. A good sense of humor will take you a long way.

Target Four: Caller, You're On The Air

Sitting in my bathrobe at home, I telephoned a friend to explain why I support animal rights. What might appear as a typical friend-to-friend conversation was really a nationally broadcast interview on radio stations in one hundred major cities. In five minutes, with almost no effort, I was able to reach millions of people with my platform. A family traveling down Route 66 heard me. A teenager in Chicago heard me. A congressman in Washington, DC, heard me. You get the picture?

Luckily for you, a lot of people forget to send news releases to radio stations. Many people believe radio shows are passé. Radio, even with its century-old roots, still reaches massive audiences; National Public Radio in the United States reaches an estimated 8 million listeners at any given point and the Canadian Broadcasting Company produces nine out of the top ten highest-rated radio programs. Radio not only generates the same responses as a television talk show, but it also requires a lot less preparation (and you don't have to worry about what you wear). And radio shows allow guests to take questions directly from listeners. To get booked on a show, send your news release, cover letter, and a few news clippings to the producer of your favorite radio program.

Getting Your Message Across on Air

- Turn off "call waiting." It seems obvious but it can be very embarrassing if, in the middle of a sentence, you hear that distinctive beep. (Call the operator to learn how.)

- Use a clear phone line. In other words, don't use a cordless phone; the static will drive the host and everyone listening crazy. Never, ever do an interview via cell phone.

- Speak slowly. You'll sound more professional, and people will have a chance to process everything you say.

- Have fun. The more personable you sound, the more receptive the audience will be.

- Be sure to remind listeners they can learn more information at your website. Do it every seven minutes or so. For example, if you're doing a thirty-minute interview, you should mention the website four times during your talk.

Target Five: Celebrities

Of all the techniques that advocacy groups use to get attention, you can almost never go wrong by tying a celebrity in with your cause.

The world is obsessed with film, sports, and TV stars. They bring a dose of glamour to a cause, get you coverage in mainstream press like People and U.S. Weekly, and grab the attention of people who would otherwise not be familiar with your cause.

How to Snare a Celebrity.

How do you get a Bruce Willis or Julia Roberts to show up at your pot luck? Well, you can't. But you may be able to get Willis or Roberts to star in a print advertisement called a Public Service Announcement on behalf of your group or even endorse a letter asking for funds. The key here is to make your request relevant to the celebrity, to make sure it is not a time-consuming commitment, and to contact the right people connected with the star to make your pitch.

To get a celebrity to sign on, there's no need to fly to Hollywood and wait outside their home. Instead, it's best to go through their handler, or management team. A celebrity usually has an agent and a publicist that shape and guide their career. Either of them can be your way to grab the star's attention.

The first thing you have to do is find out which talent agency represents the celebrity. It's usually among the big agencies in Beverly Hills: William Morris Agency, Creative Artists Agency, United Talent Agency, International Creative Management, The Gersh Agency, Artists Management Group, or Writers and Artists Agency (my agency). I would estimate they represent 80% of the A-list celebrities.

You can usually find what celebrity is repped by what agency by going on-line; fan mail is usually sent to these agencies. When you find out this information, call and ask for the name of their agent. You'll get transferred to an assistant; ask the assistant kindly who does PR for their client. Ask for a phone number, if possible.

You want to pitch to the publicist first. Their job is to get attention and manage press for their client. They are the people who get their client on magazine covers and on TV shows — to attract favorable attention. Call the PR firm and obtain the contact name and fax number; fax over your one page request. Follow-up in a week or so.

If the PR firm seems unwilling to pass on the information to their client, you can take the idea to the celebrity's talent agency. It's a time-consuming process, indeed, but getting one or two stars to sign on to your project can be a major coup for you.

A Final Thought

Media exposure is necessary to raise awareness of your issue in the community. It may seem tough at first, but your dedication and perseverance will ultimately land you and your cause in the media spotlight. And if you come across as an interesting, competent person, you'll be contacted time and time again for your input on a variety of topics. You have a voice; make it heard.

If You Liked This Chapter, You'll Love:

- Read *Guerilla P.R.* by Michael Levine (New York: Harper Collins, 1993). This is an excellent primer on public relations — my favorite PR book available on the market today.

- Visit **www.tvtalkshows.com** and **www.talkshows.about. com**. These two websites have all the news, contacts, and even media leads about nationally-distributed television talk shows. Often, producers post comments on their message boards looking for guests; you never know what you'll find.

- To see how a press release should be tailored, read news releases at **www.prnewswire.com**. The nation's top public relations firms announce product launches, events, and real news through this service. It's interesting to see how a news release can translate into print and TV coverage for a company.

- When you need to launch a comprehensive, major public relations effort, don't waste your time with directories. Vocus is a web-based public relations support company that will help you develop effective strategies by providing data bases of media contacts, lead times, and editorial calendars. Visit **www.vocus.com**.

4

generation why:

Working with Kids

*"I have found the best way to give advice to
your children is find out what they want
and then advise them to do it."*

Harry S. Truman

PART of my life is traveling all over the world to lecture at colleges, corporations, and conferences about my version of philanthropy and altruism. I've had the privilege to lecture alongside such luminaries as Archbishop Desmond Tutu, Mikhail Gorbachev, and Dr. Jane Goodall. But of all the talks I give, I must say that my speaking engagements to young people are the ones I find most rewarding.

When I was 12, an age where I was idealistic and very impressionable, I was inspired to take the path that has brought me to where I am today. That one experience — watching a television show — made me realize how important it is to connect with young people. By giving a good portion of my time to speaking to young people, sharing my thoughts, feelings, and advice on how they can get involved, I realize that I have a unique opportunity to plant a seed that may encourage them to grow up to become civic leaders. Perhaps my talk could be the "one experience" that inspires them to be the difference, too.

Working With Kids

If you want to get kids excited about acts of service, it doesn't matter if you're a parent, a concerned adult, or even a student. In fact, now couldn't be a better time for you to work with schools on creating a project that strengthens your community.

Schools across the country are now requiring students to volunteer for a set number of hours in order to graduate. While this plan has its pros and cons, it's a policy that is being enforced. No matter how you feel about "forced volunteerism," I do think this provides a good opportunity for you to bring a fun, educational, and effective project to the school.

One of the most important things you'll have to do is partner with a community-service group or non-profit organization. Most schools will not allow you, as an individual (unless you're a student), to simply create a project for the student volunteers because these institutions are concerned about the safety of their students. Having a reliable organization behind you assures the school that your project will be legitimate, well organized, and a good experience for everyone involved. Once you get a non-profit partner, come up with a project that lets students volunteer for the required number of hours. So, for example, if a student needs to do 20 hours of volunteering, create a project that takes roughly 20 hours to execute.

Keep in mind the following things when creating a project:

• Keep it fun. This doesn't mean dogwalking at the amusement park, but it should involve a good mix of different activities. Filing papers for 20 hours isn't interesting and will not likely spark much interest in the young person.

• Make it educational. What's the group's mission? If you're a conservation group, create a project where the students work on a forest that was bequeathed to the organization. Teams of students could record plants and animals living in the forest to pinpoint any rare or endangered species.

• Remember how much fun field trips were when you were in school? Change of scenery is always a good thing; the students could work in the kitchen of a nursing home, volunteer at the zoo, or even hand out organ donation forms at a concert.

For younger kids, you can visit classrooms as a guest speaker. I like talking to younger kids. Their natural honesty and curiosity make for interesting conversations. I try to keep the lecture an open dialogue, almost like a talk show format, where I speak to the kids and they are allowed to speak up whenever they feel the need to.

To talk to a group of kids at a nearby school, approach a school teacher or principal with the idea. Try to tie your talk in with a theme you're knowledgeable about and which may complement a holiday or special event. During the holiday season, for example, I often go to schools and speak to kids about sharing and altruism; my goal is for the kids to figure out that acts of selflessness can be a year-round practice, not something that's done once a year. Keep in mind that most schools won't allow political or controversial topics.

Once you've got the go-ahead, now it's time to plan your presentation. Don't overly plan it; it'll appear regimented and scripted. Instead, create a loose outline of what you'd like to talk about. Be relaxed.

Head of the Class: Grabbing their Attention

- Bring visuals. If you're talking about wildlife, arrange for rehabilitated animals to be brought in for the kids to see. Or, if you're talking about the environment, bring seeds, little pots, and some soil so the kids can plant their own wildflower seeds. Kids have short attention spans, so keep them guessing during the presentation.

- Keep them involved. Asking questions is a great way to keep the talk alive. When I asked a group of six-year-olds if they ever helped to plant a tree, I asked them to "moo." It was an odd request, and it certainly attracted attention, but it got the point home nevertheless.

- Make a mess. Growing up, one of my favorite television shows was called Double Dare — the host often had slippery, grimy goo poured all over him during the show. Kids love to see messy stuff. It's important not to get the whole class messy, but have one or two classmates get their hands dirty. When I was teaching the finer points of recycling, I took paper and water and pureed it in a blender. I poured it out and had the kids squeezing the funny-colored pulp mixture with their hands.

- Don't give out prizes. While it may seem tempting to give away candy or toys to kids, I advise against it. The idea can backfire; kids who don't win prizes will take it personally and will leave the talk with a negative impression of the event.

Getting into schools, whether it's kindergarten or the senior class, is an excellent way to get young people excited about service. While you may not change every mind in that school, you could be could be the turning point for someone — even if it's just one student, that one young person could go on to really change the world.

Getting Started: Changing School Policy

In the seventh grade, I launched a campaign in my school to give kids the option to refuse (without being penalized) to dissect an animal during class. I didn't want to impose my views on others, just to provide the option.

After an unsuccessful presentation to the school board with my resolution, I worked with lobbyists and state legislators in Pennsylvania to draft a bill that gave that option to students across the entire state. To my surprise, the bill passed and became a law just a few months after the idea was rejected by my school. In the end, the school was required to follow the law and give students in my school the option.

This was a rare case. Most of the time, you don't need to pass laws to bring reform to a school. In fact, changing school policy is easy when you plan your strategy carefully. All you need to do is speak up to the right people. But first, you need to learn what the school board is.

All of us have heard of the school board. But do we really understand *what* it is? The history of the school board in the U.S. dates back more than 200 years to the original thirteen colonies. The basic function of school boards remains the same today: to provide control over education to citizens at a point as close to the parent and child as possible. This means that the school board should represent the citizens of the school district — not just some of the citizens, but all of them. Because different citizens have different ideas about schools, this responsibility always presents a challenge.

Surprisingly, the most important job of the school board isn't to shape policy, but to employ a superintendent and to hold him or her responsible for managing the school according to the law and school board policies. It's also the job of the school board to make sure staff and teachers vigorously pursue goals set by the state and community on everything from budgets to values.

Just as with other levels of government, the school board can only take action following a majority vote at a public meeting. You, as a taxpayer, can attend those meetings — whether you're a student at the school or have kids attending the school. Anyone can attend the meetings. Board members only have the right to cast votes at those meetings. They can not speak on behalf of the board or make any decisions on their own; this is against the law.

Since the board meetings are open to the public, they must be held at a public location. There is a period of time during the meetings when citizens can speak. This is an excellent time to present new ideas, concerns, and present supporting material — polls, surveys, etc. — to the board. Since this is a public meeting, your comments are recorded and must be seriously considered.

Getting Heard

Though going to school board first is one way to express your concerns, it is not always the best way to get heard. When your concern is a district-wide policy proposal, going to the school board first may work. But if it's a smaller concern, I suggest you follow a chain of command; this process is usually easier and far more effective in getting results.

According to the U.S. National School Board Association, the best place to begin is with the person(s) directly involved. That would be the teacher where a student-related problem is involved, for example, or the principal where a school regulation or practice is what concerns you. Many larger school districts maintain community relations departments. A few employ an "ombudsman" whose job it is to represent the best interests of individual citizens and students. In any event, these people will help you or direct you to other staff members who can.

If your concerns haven't been addressed after you have worked the chain of command, take it to the next level. Bring your issue to the attention of the superintendent. When the superintendent cannot resolve your problem, that is when you should ask to be placed on the agenda for the next board meeting. If the concern is important enough to be brought before a public meeting of the full board, you'll find this approach gets a much better response than talking to an individual board member.

Lobbying Your School

Now that you understand the chain of command, you need to make sure your voice gets heard clearly. It's important to understand that your message must be honed to perfection before you speak out. A failure to do your homework ahead of time will hurt your overall chances in achieving reform.

While the process of altering school policy is very much like trying to pass a bill through Congress, there is one major difference: it is much easier to pass a school resolution than to pass a state or federal bill into law. Yes, there really is less bureaucracy and red tape at the school district level than at any other level of government. And that's good news for students and parents.

Before starting any school policy campaign, consider the following basic questions so that you'll understand your goals, your supporters, and your opponents. Be totally honest with yourself when answering these questions.

- *What is the overall goal? What do you hope to accomplish?*
  Knowing your goals ahead of time will help you define your campaign. For example, instead of saying, "I want the school to do everything possible to save the environment," a realistic goal might be "I want the school to start an office-paper recycling program."

- *Have you met with teachers and administrators who have the power to change the questionable school policy?*
It is much easier to work from the bottom up on school campaigns. Sometimes changes can be made at a non-administrative level. For example, a student's effort to implement an HIV/AIDS awareness campaign could be done through the school nurse, who may already be teaching a school-wide health class, rather than going through the bureaucratic administrative process.

- *Who are your supporters? The student body? Teachers? A special-interest group?*
Knowing your supporters ahead of time will help you recruit people farther down the road. Instead of scrambling for help at the last minute, keep an army of people on hand for immediate use. It might be a good idea to create a flow-chart listing names identifying the unique good qualities each brings to the table.

- *Who are your opponents? The student body? Teachers? A special-interest group?*
Keep track of your opposing forces. Some people may try to infiltrate your group in an effort to strengthen their case against your efforts. You should develop a plan to respond to the concerns and actions of any opposing groups or people.

- *What are your personal strengths? Are you a good speaker? Writer?*
Use your talents to further your efforts. If you excel at media relations, work on getting coverage in all media outlets. If you are an exceptional writer, write an article for the school newspaper and a letter to the editor of your local newspaper.

• *What is your time frame?*

Whatever your goals, a time frame is critical to any campaign. Knowing how much time you have to successfully launch and execute your plans will be key in developing a strategy.

Now it's time to develop a plan of action.

Follow the chain of command and express your concerns to the right people. Present ideas and solutions. Use visuals. Don't forget to approach people who aren't normally approached with new ideas. For example, if you want vegetarian options on the cafeteria menu every day, arrange a meeting with the cafeteria supervisor. They usually purchase food for the school and could order some veggie burgers next time around. If you want a composting program, meet with the head groundskeeper.

Writing a Resolution

If you don't have any luck meeting with people in the chain of command, you'll need to write a resolution to present to the school board. In short, a resolution is like a declaration, citing facts, incidents and a solution that the school should adopt. There's no real boiler plate outline that you have to use, so feel free to come up with your own.

Here's a sample resolution that I used in my school. A couple of awkward words that are used:

• **Whereas**: In view of the fact that…
• **Resolved**: Formally decided.

How to Create a Resolution

RESOLUTION NO.: _____

PROHIBITING THE PENALIZING OF STUDENTS FOR REFUSAL OF DISSECTING AN ANIMAL IN GOVERNOR MIFFLIN PUBLIC SCHOOLS

- WHEREAS, the Governor Mifflin Board of Education fully endorses scientific education and presentations in the classrooms; and
- WHEREAS, the Board is sensitive to student and parent objections to animal dissection in the classroom; and
- WHEREAS, the Board fully recognizes the rights of students to an education that does not violate their religious and ethical beliefs and value systems; and
- WHEREAS, the Medical Research Modernization Committee, the Physicians' Committee for Responsible Medicine, and the Humane Society of the United States have provided curricula that teach children about the biology and physiology of animals without requiring the death of animals; and
- WHEREAS, modern tools of research such as computer-assisted mannequins, computer programs, mathematical and physical models, and videotapes have been devised that eliminate the need to use animals; and
- WHEREAS, requiring students to dissect animals tends to desensitize or revolt children rather than educate them and also has the unwanted effect of discouraging sensitive students from pursuing careers in science; now, therefore, be it

- RESOLVED, that the dissection of animals shall be an option to students at all course levels in Governor Mifflin Public Schools.

Before the school board meeting, recruit parents, neighbors, and students who are sympathetic to your cause. The funny thing about most school board meetings is that they are rarely attended by the public. For a while, I was the only person who attended them in my district. So you can imagine how urgent it might seem if twenty, ten or even five people come to support your presentation.

Presentation Night

Don't read word for word from a written speech: it's boring. Instead, put the points you want to make in outline form and elaborate on the spot. Speak from the heart and be genuine. Be adamant, passionate, and staunch in your beliefs. Have other students and parents speak in support of your resolution. Be understanding of the school's concerns but remain strong and assertive. Answer their questions in a nonthreatening, non-defensive, intelligent manner. Don't be vulgar in your language even if a board member behaves condescendingly toward you. If you act inappropriately, you risk losing the support you might have had. If you sense that the board will not support your resolution immediately, encourage them to take the time to consider your proposal and ask them to decide its status at the next meeting.

If your resolution doesn't pass, don't worry. This is the time to compromise with the school board — to find some common ground where you can achieve some of your goals while they keep some of their outdated policy. You're looking for ways to create a dialogue. Remember, your school board is made of elected officials who are neighbors; they share your concerns and want to make sure the school is run in a manner that best reflects the community and the kids at the school.

- *Keep the communication open.* Make it a point to talk to individual school board members. Keep attending meetings. Add your concerns to the agenda for future meetings, making sure that you bring fresh, relevant news each time.

• *Say thank you.* Be sure to thank each school board member, the principal, superintendent, assistant superintendent, reporters who covered your story, and students who rallied behind you from the start.

• *Establish the compromise.* For example, if the school board has agreed to give students the option to refuse animal dissections *only* if they request this at the beginning of the year, sign up as many students as possible at the start of the first semester. This way, the school board will see an overwhelming demand for the program and will likely pass your complete resolution giving students a year-round option to refuse dissections.

• *Implement the idea.* For example, if you wanted the school to start a recycling program and they refused to do so, create a pilot program to show how effective and easily executed it can be. On paper, a lot of ideas seem cumbersome and difficult. If you and some volunteers can execute a project and break down prejudices, then the board might be more inclined to support you.

• *Find supporters.* Contact like-minded national organizations, societies, and prominent change agents to support your effort. Have them send letters to the school superintendent, endorsing your resolution. And, if possible, have them provide positive comments to the school board as well.

• *Advertise in the school.* Look for ways to advertise your campaign in school publications. Does the school's fall play have ad space available in the program? How about the school newspaper? Football program? Orchestra performance handout? Be creative, imaginative, and spread the word. These ads are often very inexpensive and can hit the core audience effectively. Don't be worried about overexposure: that should be the least of your concerns.

PTA

The national PTA is the largest volunteer child advocacy organization in the United States. With nearly 6.5 million members working in 26,000 local chapters across the country, this organization of parents and teachers makes sure that kids are getting the highest quality of education possible at their schools.

Almost every school district in the U.S. has a PTA. To find out how and when you can attend meetings, simply call the school. In my alma mater, the PTA was responsible for creative fund-raising projects, and even hosted special events to deter kids from drinking and driving on prom night. PTAs vary in size and scope from school to school, but they have an excellent "in" at most schools and can be a great way to bring change. You can learn anything and everything about the PTA at **www.pta.org**

A Final Thought

Changing school policy is a good way to learn civics. Whether you are in the community or in the school, you have the right to speak up whenever a policy infringes on people's rights or is ethically objectionable. Don't be intimidated by school officials: it's your world too.

If You Liked This Chapter, You'll Love:

• Learn everything about school boards, including your rights as a taxpayer and more, at the National Association of School Board's website at **www.nasb.org**. In Canada, visit the Canadian School Boards Association at **www.cdnsba.org**.

• For a free guide to your First Amendment rights, contact the Freedom Forum by calling toll-free **1 (800) 815•5335** or write: **1101 Wilson Boulevard, Arlington, VA 22209**, or find them on-line at **www.freedomforum.org**.

• Bookmark **www.bolt.com**. This leading on-line website for teens features an entire channel devoted to news and issues, including updates on student rights and how students can "come together and unite to be active in the pursuit of our common goal, freedom for all youth."

• Help wire schools and assist schools to take full advantage of technology and the Internet. NetDay's mission is to help educators think beyond the technical issues to a consideration of educational benefits, creating environments where the magic of learning is enhanced through the use of technological resources. Find them at **www.netday.org**.

5
understanding government:

If Mr. Smith Goes to Washington, So Can You

*"A government is the only known vessel
that leaks from the top."*

James Reston

'VE always believed that if you want to make a big difference —
to have a colossal effect on the world — you need to pass a law.
That way, despite what your detractors might say, you'll still
have the law on your side. Granted, it's not the one and only
answer to reform, but it sure goes a long way. When thousands of
acres of rare forest are threatened with being destroyed forever,
for example, there are two options: one, buy the forest, or two,
have the state or federal government pass a law that sets aside
funds to preserve it. Unless you've got hundreds of millions of
dollars to spare, the second option is the most logical. As a
taxpayer, you have a right to help decide where your money
should be spent.

Lobbying

If you're like most people, you probably have a preconceived
notion that a lobbyist is someone who works for big businesses to

Pop Quiz.

*Which of the following
is a lobbyist:
the distinguished man
in the three-piece suit
working for the tobacco industry?
the female college graduate working
for the Children's Defense Fund?
or the radical hippie
chaining himself to the flagpole
outside the White House
to protest nuclear weapons?
The answer is (drumroll, please):
all of the above.*

make their wallets fatter and their influence greater. But not all lobbyists represent corporate greed: many work for non-profit groups and others voluntarily lobby to support personal, closely held convictions. And yes, even the radical hippie chained to the flagpole is a lobbyist: he's just bringing attention to an issue in an unconventional, attention-grabbing way. Effective? Well, that's for the president of the United States to decide.

Unlike public relations and fund-raising, lobbying wasn't one of those skills that I had a great fondness for. In fact, growing up, I hesitated to get involved because lobbying my elected officials seemed like a complicated act I would never be able to master. But I soon learned that lobbying is nothing more than meeting with your elected officials and trying to convince them to support your point of view.

My first lobbying experience grew from a personal concern. It all started on a cool fall day in Green Hills, Pennsylvania, when I was standing in a field of pumpkins looking around for the perfect jack-o'-lantern. As my friends ran around the three-acre field looking for the best pumpkin, I picked a shiny apple from the orchard next to the pumpkin patch. I ate it — not thinking about any possible pesticides, herbicides, or insecticides that might've been sprayed on it. After all, how much harm could one apple do?

By that night my skin had broken out in an itchy bright red rash covering my face, neck, and back. I wasn't physically sick, fortunately, but I looked so hideous that my mother refused to allow me to attend school for several days. Could it be from the apple? Was it from being exposed to pesticides? I thought so, but had no concrete proof. But if my intuition was telling me anything, it was that there was something on that apple that made me sick.

Several months later, after my apple phobia had passed, I was approached by my friend Carla about lobbying for a Pennsylvania bill that would require schools to limit the use of pesticides and herbicides on school grounds. It was written to protect allergy-sensitive students from being harmed by chemicals like grass fertilizer and ant repellent. This time, instead of making an excuse to back out, I wanted to help. I now knew from my own experience the dangers of pesticides and what they can do to a person.

When I told Carla my apple-eating-and-rash story, she was intrigued. In fact, she was so interested that she booked me to speak at a news conference in Harrisburg, Pennsylvania, about my experience with food and chemical fertilizers and pesticides.

It was my very first lobbying experience. And with very little knowledge of how government worked (I didn't even know who my legislators were), I was scared. I wasn't a scientist or an expert in chemical fertilizers; I was just a regular teenager who got sick from eating a treated apple. To my surprise, after nervously sharing my five-minute story at the news conference, reporters and legislators were interested in what I had to say. That night, on the evening news, thousands of families across Pennsylvania saw and heard my speech urging support for this legislation. It was the easiest thing I ever did, but it achieved the greatest result: it convinced several doubtful legislators to support the bill. Since that day, I've been in constant contact with my legislators about issues that concern me.

Lobbying 101

Lobbying is a long-standing practice in state and federal legislatures. Lobbyists — representatives of both private and public groups — attempt to influence government policy in favor of the tenets of their organization. For example, a lobbyist hired by the retail industry might lobby to stop Congress from raising the minimum wage. On the other hand, a lobbyist representing a union of retail workers would try to convince Congress to raise the minimum wage. And because they can provide substantial donations to an official's reelection campaign and/or represent a significant number of registered voters in a legislator's district, lobbyists work from a position of strength. They keep legislators informed of their organization's position on all pending legislation within their field of interest. But the most important lobbyist is the voter, and legislators listen to our voice, whether it comes through letters, e-mails, faxes, or phone calls. Our elected officials want to make sure they represent the views of us, their constituents, as well as possible.

There are three main types of lobbyists.

- **CORPORATE LOBBYISTS**. These people are hired by corporations to fight or support laws that affect their employers' livelihood, as in oil company lobbyists working for weaker environmental regulations. They are usually full-time employees who routinely meet with legislators and sometimes give substantial monetary "gifts" to the legislator's reelection fund as a show of support. In return for their gift, they hope the congressperson will vote for laws that help their corporation.

- **SPECIAL INTEREST LOBBYISTS**. These are employed by non-profit organizations. For example, lobbyists for the National Rifle Association (NRA) try to protect the rights of gun owners and hunters. The lobbyists hired by Handgun Control, on the other hand, work for stronger gun control, while the Fund for Animals works to protect animals by fighting the interest of hunters. There are thousands of registered, non-profit lobbyists working to influence laws affecting everything from the rights of children to the rights of whales. Like corporate lobbyists, special-interest groups who use lobbyists often donate money to legislators' reelection coffers through a special arm of the group called a political action committee, or PAC. Since they cannot use regular funds to support legislators due to non-profit tax laws, these groups form a PAC funded by private contributions for the sole purpose of giving monetary gifts to legislators. They also offer cooperative congresspeople something even more appealing – the votes of the members of their organizations. Groups like the Sierra Club, with 400,000 members, and the Humane Society of the United States with millions of members, often have clout among congresspeople for this reason alone.

- **VOLUNTEER LOBBYISTS**. These people are not paid for their services and are usually active for only one reason: they feel passionate about their cause. In their spare time, these ordinary citizens use grassroots tactics – lobbying that does not involve big sums of money, but instead uses personal actions such as letter writing campaigns and press conferences – to influence legislation at the state and federal level just as paid lobbyists do. For example, a mother who lost her son to a drunk driver might lobby for stiffer drunk-driving laws. This is the type of lobbying you can learn how to do.

Breaking Down Preconceived Notions

Lobbying is perceived as a difficult thing to do. It's not.

My first lobbying experiences occurred when I was just a teenager. I often took days off school, taking a 6 a.m. bus to my state capitol to spend the day pressing the flesh with legislators. It was an unusual experience for me – not the actual process of

> Lobbying is just a technical term
> for the simple act
> of expressing your views
> to a congressperson.
> In my opinion,
> it is one of the easiest ways
> a person can make a difference,
> so it's worth your time
> to give it a try.

lobbying, but being the only teenager actually working there, rather than one who was taking the hour-long tour.

I will admit that, at first, I was scared to meet with my legislators, worrying that my comments might hurt my cause instead of helping it. But unfounded fears have a way of dissipating all on their own, and the more meetings I had, the more confident I felt about my lobbying abilities. My opinions on pending legislation had a profound effect on the voting records of my legislators. The entire lobbying experience was like a meeting with a friend. I also discovered legislators really do care about the feelings of their constituents. Even though I personally couldn't vote at the time, I was still a very influential lobbyist, because as president of Earth 2000, I was in contact with thousands of teens throughout Pennsylvania who had parents and older siblings who did vote. My lobbyist friend Laura summed it up best when she said, "No politician wants to be known as the legislator who made a group of kids cry."

Back in my school, I started recruiting other young people to come with me to the state capitol. At one point, we actually took the term lobbying literally: we set-up a booth right in the lobby of the Capitol building, handing out brochures and pamphlets to passers-by. Many of these people included politicians and the press who found it unusual to see a group of teenagers being so knowledgeable about pending environmental legislation.

As more and more of our peers got involved, we became aware of how important voting really is. When a local state representative refused to change his views on a bill, we rallied together in our small town, where only a tiny percentage of people would normally turn out to vote, and started swaying even hard-core Republicans to switch their vote. It was amazing to see so many of my peers feel passionate about politics. Today, voting is still a major priority for all of us; I've been known to hop on a red-eye flight back from the West Coast to cast my vote in New York (when I forgot to secure an absentee ballot).

I think schools should abandon the traditional route of a class field trip to teach students about politics and our government. Instead, young people should research legislation and bills that are pending on issues they care about, such as gun control, the environment, and health care. Schools should set up meetings with groups of young people, sit down with them, and have an unrehearsed conversation with them. Keep it real. I've always believed that when you take a hard-to-understand topic like lobbying and present it in a straightforward, understandable format, people will grasp the idea immediately. Imagine the possibilities if every young person had a one-on-one experience with the politicians.

The Lingo of Lobbyists: A Dictionary for Novices

As a lobbyist, there are some basic terms that you should know. These are words commonly used by elected officials, their staffs, and lobbyists. Don't use them just to impress a friend at a party; make them part of your lobbying vocabulary:

Act: A bill that has been passed by both houses and becomes law.

Bill: A proposed law introduced in either the House or Senate.

Committee: Workshops composed of legislators who study new bills, dissect them to find problems, and hear concerns from lobbyists, constituents, and other legislators.

Constituent: A public citizen in a legislator's district.

District: A territory of the state that has one state senator and one state representative to represent its interest in the state legislature. Federal districts are larger and have one federal representative. Every state has two federal senators.

Filibuster: To deliberately take advantage of the freedom of debate — a law which allows a legislator unlimited time to debate a bill before a vote — in order to delay the vote on a bill.

Impeachment: A proceeding brought against an elected official for the purpose of removing that official for misbehavior in office.

Non-partisan: Not influenced by political party bias.

PACs: Political Action Committees; special-interest groups (or the separate political arm of a non-profit organization) who lobby legislators and who may sometimes make campaign contributions to political candidates.

Resolution: A form of written proposal used to make declarations, state policies, or announce decisions when a bill or some other form of legislative action is not required. For example, a legislator who wants to proclaim Pennsylvania's support for rainforest preservation needs only a resolution to get the proclamation approved. The difference between a bill and resolution is clear: a resolution does not become a law. It is, however, a way for the legislature to make a statement about its views on an issue.

Table:	To postpone action or debate on a bill. If a legislator has a special interest in a certain bill (e.g., a bill that would force cattle ranchers to pay higher taxes in a district which has more cows than people), the legislator would try to table discussion – and therefore stall action – until he or she could find a way to gain support.
Veto:	The power of the president of the United States and each state's governor to reject a bill that has already passed both legislative houses.

Doing Your Homework

Before you become a grassroots lobbyist, you need to understand the basic process of how an idea becomes a law. There are many steps in the lawmaking process, which is designed to question the need for and the effectiveness of a proposed law. The deliberate slowness allows for open discussion and provides many opportunities for the general public to influence the shape of the final legislation. Here's how an idea becomes a law at the state level.

Take a field trip to your state capital and tour the capitol building. (Call first for times, dates, restrictions, etc.) The tour will familiarize you with the layout of the building, the historical aspects of government, and the workings of government in your state. It won't answer every question you have about government, but it's a good way to get your feet wet.

First, a member of the general assembly – the official name for the entire body of all state legislatures – writes a bill. The legislator now looks for other legislators to co-sponsor the bill so it will have a better chance of passing. It's like the bandwagon theory: the more co-sponsors a bill has, the better chance it has of gaining support because of internal peer pressure.

The bill is then introduced to the general assembly and sent to the appropriate committee for review and public distribution, which is the process of informing the general public about the pending legislation.

Once committee members have reviewed the bill — and after hearing the concerns of constituents, lobbyists, and other legislators — they will either leave the bill alone or amend (change) it. Changes will be made if the majority of the committee feels clarifying measures or words need to be added. These changes are made to solve any problems the original bill did not address. The bill can also be tabled, which is the process of postponing legislation — in other words, killing the bill.

Once out of the committee, the bill is reintroduced, with its changes, in the Senate or House, depending on where the bill originated, for vote. For our purposes, let's just say it originated in the Senate. The bill is then voted on by the Senate.

After the bill passes the Senate by majority vote, it is transmitted to the House, where it is assigned to a House committee. The House committee may make changes or table the bill. Any changes made by the House must be approved by the Senate. If the Senate approves them, then the bill is voted on by the House. If the changes are not approved by the Senate, then further changes can be made by both sides until the bill is acceptable to both the House and the Senate.

If the bill passes both houses, it is signed by the president of the Senate and the speaker of the House. It is then transmitted to the governor for his consideration.

If the governor signs the bill, it becomes law. If the governor rejects the bill, it is returned to the house of origin with the governor's reason for veto. The veto can be overturned with a two-thirds majority vote of each house.

If the governor takes no action on the bill within ten calendar days after he/she has received it, and the general assembly is still in session, it automatically becomes law.

The official certified copy of each bill approved by the governor is placed in the custody of the secretary of state, given an act number, and filed with the state department.

It's a complicated process, designed to allow for checks and balances, comments, and review by other government officials and the public. Often, an idea can become a law in a matter of days while others may take years or never make it at all.

Hard to Follow?

If, after reading the above (dare I say) simplified version of how a bill becomes a law, you're still a bit confused about the legislative process, don't worry. I've been lobbying for several years now, and I'm still learning how government works. All you really need is a *basic* understanding of the bill process, to know who your state and federal legislators are, and what bill in your field of interest is being circulated among congresspeople in Washington and in your state capital.

In the Commonwealth of Pennsylvania, about 5,000 bills are introduced every two years. Amazing. And every day, bills are made into law without the public taking much notice. There are hundreds of regulations passed every year, many of which go completely unnoticed by ordinary people like you and me. We read about a new law in the Sunday newspaper only after it's too late to take any action. What's a frustrated, ordinary citizen to do?

There are several steps you can take to stay informed about pending bills at the state and federal levels. If you are already working for a special cause, you can join a like-minded special interest group that will keep you informed of bills on that subject. Usually, these organizations will send you a quarterly or monthly newsletter listing the pending bills, including the bill's identification number and even the names of the legislators who either support or oppose the bill. They do a pretty good job monitoring the comings and goings in government. There's even a long-distance phone carrier who can keep you updated on new and pending federal legislation. Here's a sample of five national political action organizations:

- **THE FUND FOR ANIMALS**. This national anti-hunting organization has full-time lobbyists working at both the state and national levels on issues concerning animals, specifically the hunting and trapping of them. They publish an annual report that ranks federal officials on their voting record, and also produce action alerts and newsletters for their members, notifying them of current legislative efforts. Contact: **The Fund for Animals, 850 Sligo Avenue, #300, Silver Spring, MD 20910**. You can contact them at **www.fund.org**

- **CHILDREN'S DEFENSE FUND**. This national non-profit group exists to provide a strong and effective voice for all children in America, "who cannot vote, lobby, or speak for themselves." The office of government affairs tracks key legislative proposals addressing children's issues: health care, child care, and Head Start, to name a few. Members receive action alerts on issues concerning child advocacy. Contact: **Children's Defense Fund, 25 E Street, NW, Washington, DC 20001**, or on-line at **www.childrens defense.org**

- **LEAGUE OF CONSERVATION VOTERS**. This is a non-partisan, national political campaign committee that actively promotes the election of public officials who work for a healthy environment. They evaluate environmental voting records of congressional members and presidential candidates. The highest score, 100 percent, indicates an elected official who is a staunch protector of the environment. Contact: **League of Conservation Voters, 1150 Connecticut Avenue, Suite 201, Washington, DC 20036.**

• **PUBLIC CITIZEN.** This is a national organization working to fight the "special interests" of powerful corporations in government. Founded in 1971 by Ralph Nader, consumer activist and 1996 Green Party presidential candidate, Public Citizen consists of ordinary citizens banding together to defend democracy and to protect themselves from the tyranny of the rich and powerful. Contact: **Public Citizen, 2000 P Street, NW, Washington, DC 20036**, on-line at **www.citizen.org**

• **WORKING ASSETS.** This is the nation's leading *socially responsible* long-distance phone service company that not only gives a percentage of your monthly phone bill to non-profit groups such as Greenpeace and Planned Parenthood but also keeps you informed of upcoming bills where your voice can influence the outcome of political and social issues. Each telephone bill (printed on recycled paper) highlights a specific bill in Congress that may interest you. Working Assets even foots the bill for your phone call to your legislator in Washington. Not bad for a phone company. Contact: **Working Assets, 1 (800)-788•8588**, or visit their website: **www.wald.com**

Once you've discovered a bill that concerns you, you can receive copies of it by contacting your elected official's district office (be sure to contact state officials for state bills, federal officials for federal bills), or call the House Document Office for copies. Be sure to have the bill number available (usually stated in a group's action alert). If you don't know the bill number, call the legislator's office for assistance.

Getting Started as a Lobbyist

First, make a list of your state and federal legislators. If you don't know who they are, contact your local League of Women Voters (LWV). The LWV is a U.S. national organization working to promote active participation of citizens in government. They can provide you with a list of your elected officials, including their addresses, phone and fax numbers, and other useful information. The LWV, which is on-line at **www.lwv.org**, can help you with voter registration as well as general questions about the political process. You can also contact the chief clerk's office in your state capital for a complete list of current state officials.

In Canada, every telephone book has a "Blue Pages" section that lists government departments at the municipal, provincial, and federal level with a 1 (800) number to call for phone and fax numbers for elected members. If you are writing to a federal elected official or the prime minister, postage is free.

It's Meeting Time

Once you have a list of your elected officials, you need to make appointments with them. Setting up a meeting is easy: call the legislator's local district office (look in the blue pages of your phone book). Legislators commute regularly between their main and district offices, so setting up a meeting date shouldn't be difficult.

All you need is a fifteen-minute appointment, and be flexible on times and dates. Be ready to give a general explanation as to why you are requesting a meeting. That's all it takes.

Once you have the appointment with your elected official (or with the legislative aide, when lobbying a federal official), you need to focus on which issues you will discuss. Here are some ideas:

- **BILLS.** Be specific regarding your position on a pending piece of legislation by stating your opposition or support.

- **GENERAL ISSUES.** Give your general feelings about a topic – such as gun control, animal rights, and welfare. Ask your legislator to keep your views in mind when voting on these issues.

- **FEEDBACK ON PAST VOTES.** If a legislator voted against a bill you favored, discuss why he or she voted against it. Doing so might convince the official to vote differently in the future.

How to Meet and Greet Your Politican

Be relaxed and calm during the meeting. This is your opportunity to express yourself. Many legislators enjoy this give-and-take with their constituents: it's a refreshing change from the daily schmoozing with trained lobbyists. Be honest, clear, and to the point about your feelings. Be forthright about your stand on a bill or issue: right off the bat, say, "I support the Clean Water Act." Get your opinion heard loud and clear. Here are some tips for a successful meeting:

- **DRESS APPROPRIATELY.** Make sure you wear clean, nice-looking clothes. While it may seem silly to dress up for a meeting with your elected official, you won't earn respect by wearing jeans and a t-shirt.

- **BRING A FRIEND OR GROUP OF FRIENDS.** Having other concerned citizens with you will show there is additional support in the community. Be sure there is a general consensus as to what the meeting is about and who is to be the spokesperson. Without an appointed spokesperson, you run the risk of having chaos and misrepresentation at the meeting.

If you bring a group of people, be sure to send out a news release to the local media. Grassroots lobbying by private citizens might interest some journalists. If you plan to meet your legislator at the main office in the capitol building, you can send out a statewide release in a few minutes. Your state capitol has a press office where journalists representing major newspaper and television and radio outlets receive daily news releases. The morning of your appointment, drop off fifty copies of your news release to inform every major media outlet of your lobbying efforts. It could lead to statewide exposure.

- **KEEP THE MEETING SHORT**. No meeting should last longer than fifteen minutes. But if your legislator insists on ending the meeting in under five minutes, tell him or her that you deserve at least a few minutes of time. You did, after all, take time out of your busy schedule to meet with your elected official. You – and your friends and family – do vote.

- **BRING THE BILL WITH YOU**. Some legislators might try to get out of taking a stand on a bill by saying they do not have a copy handy. Be thorough (and annoyingly efficient) by bringing two copies of the bill with you. (Use the resources mentioned earlier to get copies of the bill.)

- **USE GRAPHICS**. Bring photographs or letters from people in the community supporting your efforts. For example, if you want to save an historic landmark, bring photos of it and supportive letters from voters in the district.

- **HAVE FUN AT THE MEETING.** Be creative. Never threaten. Ask questions. Most important, stress the importance to you of your issue or your position on a bill. Ask for a follow-up meeting or reply.

- **AFTER THE MEETING.** A few days after your meeting, send a thank-you note to your legislator. Mention you look forward to receiving his or her support for your issue and would appreciate any specific feedback on the actions their office has taken following your meeting. Leave a phone number and mailing address so the legislator's aide can contact you with an update.

Getting Heard

Can't take time off of work to meet with your legislator? No problem. You can still get your opinion heard by devoting a few minutes every week to creating a friendly relationship with your legislator. This is not as powerful as a face-to-face meeting, but can be very effective in influencing the way your legislator votes.

- **MAKE A PHONE CALL.** Ever call a company's 800 number to complain about a product? Do the same with your legislator and leave a constituent comment. A one-sentence comment such as "I would like Senator Smith to support Bill Number 379, the Clean Air Law" is all an elected official needs to hear to keep track of who supports or opposes a bill in his district. Your one call could make the difference. Also, leave your name and address for a response from the legislator.

- **FAX OR MAIL A LETTER.** Get this: every time you send a letter to your legislator, it is considered that your view equals that of ten other constituents in your district. Even more amazing: a letter to the president of the United

States equals the same views of one hundred other citizens! Believe me, your letters really do count.

- **E-MAIL**. Don't you love technology? Our elected officials are now on-line. You can check their websites to catch up on their voting record and leave comments at their e-mail addresses. Call the local district offices for their website and e-mail addresses. To get your e-mail campaign started, leave a message for the president of the United States at: **president@whitehouse.gov** or e-mail the vice president at: **vicepresident@whitehouse.gov**. Visit the League of Women Voter's website to find out the URL addresses and e-mails for your other elected officials.

In Canada, you can contact the prime minister through the official website: **www.pm.gc.ca** or via e-mail at **pm@pm.gc.ca**. The website also provides links to every major government office in Canada, with e-mail and postal mailing addresses.

Isn't lobbying easy? The process of influencing legislation on the local, state, and federal level is one every concerned citizen needs to understand and participate in. We have the power to make our opinions heard on issues we care about. By creating a positive working relationship with your legislators, you can become a constant influential force in their lives. Without your vote, they know they'll be out of a job come election time. Make your legislators aware of your beliefs, your needs, and your thoughts – and hold them accountable for their actions.

If You Liked This Chapter, You'll Love:

- Join Common Cause, a national, non-partisan lobbying group working to bring people across the country together in an effort to lobby elected officials on issues of mutual concern. Issues where their influence has made a difference include winning passage of a comprehensive ban on lobbying gifts, establishing lobby disclosure for legislators, and pressing for civil and equal rights for all citizens. For a free membership form, write: **Common Cause, 2030 M Street, NW, Washington, DC 20036-3380** or visit **www.commoncause.org**.

• Get involved with 20/20 Vision. They make grassroots change simple for busy people by giving citizens the information they need to get involved in a wide range of progressive issues, such as conserving the environment, shifting military spending to domestic needs, stopping handgun violence, and getting money out of our campaign process. Their once-a-month alerts (e-mail or snail mail) tell you how to quickly and easily contact politicians and corporate officials to let them know your views on an urgent issue. Go on-line at **www.2020 vision.org**.

• Find the chapter of the League of Women Voters closest to your community. Not just for women, the LWV works to educate people about the voting process and to make sure that ordinary people can speak up and be heard. Learn who your elected officials are, where and how to vote, and where to register. Go to **www.lwv.org**.

6

bringing everyone together:

Event Planning for Dummies

*"Never give a party if you will be
the most innteresting person there."*

Mickey Friedman

HAVE you ever been caught up in the moment and thought, "Maybe I'll host a small dinner party this Saturday." And after you have e-mailed all your friends and family to attend your "small" dinner party, did it get to the point where you felt like it was going to blow up in your face? The food, the drinks, the parking situation, and a million other tiny problems arise just minutes before the first guest arrives. But somehow everything pulls together and you have a fabulous time.

Bringing people together in the name of charity can conjure up the same stressful feelings. It can be a fantastic experience that motivates people, inspires new ideas, and raises lots of money for charity. Or it can be a disaster: cold food, weather-related problems, and even angry confrontations with people. I'm sure you've experienced one or two blunders like this at some time.

Whatever your trepidations, special events, when organized properly, can be a great way to get change going. The key is to keep it simple and always focus on the goal: you're here to make a difference.

Party Time

Whenever I want to do something, but am unsure how to do it, I always turn to my trusty yellow pages. Charter a bus to a beach cleanup? Look under transportation. Recycle an old brass bed? Scrap metal recycling. You get the idea.

> *If you asked me*
> *which single book*
> *I would bring*
> *to a deserted island,*
> *it wouldn't be a great novel*
> *or tome full of inspiring words.*
> *It would be the phone book.*

One of the most memorable events that I ever coordinated was when I was sixteen years old. I decided that our organization hadn't done enough hands-on activities — things like cleaning beaches, planting trees — and was focusing too heavily on legislative and legal matters. We were, after all, a group of teenagers. So to celebrate our successes and have some fun, I decided to organize a beach cleanup.

Reading, Pennsylvania is nowhere near a beach. We decided to visit New Jersey and spend the morning cleaning the beaches and the afternoon having lunch and plain ol' fun. But after calling some private charter busing companies, the cost of having a private driver take us to New Jersey and back for the day was prohibitive. But like any well-run organization, we had a Plan B.

"Why not Atlantic City?," someone asked. And why not, I thought. While it may seem like an odd choice for a beach cleanup, the beaches did need some cleaning, there were plenty of fun and interesting activities in the area, and — let's face it — there were plenty of public bathrooms for a group of soda-chugging teenagers to use. With daily buses leaving Reading for Atlantic City, and tickets selling for a song, we made it a plan.

Like a parent, I planned ahead: my group of twenty "kids" would need protective gloves, bottled water, trash bags, a first aid kit, and sanitary "towelettes" to keep our hands clean after our good deed.

When we arrived in Atlantic City, we spent a few hours picking up trash. The odd part was that the beaches were empty: everyone was gambling. So despite a busy boardwalk, it felt like we had a private beach all to ourselves. And with public trash cans placed throughout the beach, we found we could fill up our trash bags with refuse, and just deposit them in the trash cans. The whole experience was not only fulfilling, but it was also a cinch to do. Miles of beaches ended up being cleaned. The whole area looked so spotless that even the hard-to-impress members of the group were taken back by our achievement.

We spent the remaining part of the day exploring the boardwalk: getting our futures read by a bad fortune teller, playing in vintage arcades, eating boardwalk food. What made the whole experience so memorable was that we not only achieved something immediate by cleaning the beach, but we also renewed our spirit by remembering why we became concerned about the planet in the first place. This little day trip was like a corporate retreat and, from what I saw in the coming weeks, recharged everyone to continue to battle to save our planet.

Getting People Out To Your Event

Have you ever thrown a party and worried that no one would show up? It's a fear lots of people have about hosting charitable special events. To get people to attend your event, the most important thing you need to do is to get the word out.

You cannot advertise, market, or talk too much about your event. Here are some ideas to advertise your event that do not cost a lot.

- *Newspapers.* Send an announcement to all the local newspapers about your event as soon as you start planning it. Try to get your event mentioned in a calendar of events in the paper at least two months before the date. Push again for another mention one month before and also the week of the event. Don't be afraid to call the newspaper directly and ask how they'd like to receive the information; some editors prefer e-mail now, so it pays to call.

- *Announcements.* Make fliers on 8.5 by 11 inch paper and have them distributed at offices, schools, and relevant special events. Don't waste your time leaving them in mailboxes (which is illegal in the United States), on car windshields, or doorstops. Ask your friends to place announcements in corporate newsletters, in non-profit group mailings, and over the public address system at secondary and higher education schools.

- *E-mail.* Most groups keep their members up-to-date via e-mail. Obtain mailing lists from friends and like-minded organizations. Be sure to tailor e-mail lists so they don't appear to be "spam" e-mails. For example, if Mary Smith shares her e-mail list, put in the subject line, "Mary Smith Wants to Invite You."

- *Book a Smaller Venue.* While this isn't a way to get people out, per say, it's a smart way to make people feel they are part of a successful event. Instead of booking a gymnasium that can hold a thousand people, book something that holds fewer people than you anticipate. The reality is there will probably be fewer people than you anticipate who will show up at your event for a variety of reasons: weather, traffic, outright forgetfulness. Sparsely-filled rooms make an event appear less successful; a room with an overflow section gives the impression of a successful event — and everyone will leave thinking that it is. It also looks better in photos.

Volunteers Just Wanna Have Fun

Putting together a special event for your friends and neighbors can be a lot of fun. There's no need to put together the complicated, star-studded kind of party you see in the pages of *Vanity Fair*. That's why I'm giving some easy-to-replicate, small-scale special events which will raise awareness of your cause and promote pride in your community – and which you can actually do. I tell you *who* you should contact, *when* to start organizing, and *what* are the absolute must-do's. And remember, don't let the hard work associated with organizing special events overwhelm you.

Outdoor Events

Oh, the great outdoors with its babbling brooks and chirping birds. What a shame we spend so much time indoors, at shopping malls, in office buildings, at home, and locked in our cars. Sad, isn't it? It doesn't have to be. Organize an outdoor special event and introduce people to the lush grass, towering trees, and soft sand of the great outdoors.

- **PICNICS.** Whether you want to celebrate a campaign win or to bring people together for new member orientation, a picnic is a great outdoor event. All you need is some food, a few drinks, and a little music. But remember, it's not just a party: the event should have a purpose. Take a few minutes during the event to talk about future campaigns and to congratulate any members who are doing an outstanding job. And in case it rains, always have a rain date. If the morning of the event looks overcast, postpone it.

  Who: Contact the park manager and ask about permit requirements for your picnic; you may not need one. Also, send invitations to guests.

When: Contact everyone about the picnic at least a month ahead of time. Make sure they RSVP!

What: Bring food. Try to receive in-kind donations of food from local grocers and bakers. Be careful about alcohol; there might be an "open bottle" law in your community. Call city hall to find out.

• **CLEANUPS**. Environmentalists aren't the only ones doing cleanups. Everyone is pitching in today to pick up litter from beaches, forests, and highways. Cleanups bond people together for one simple reason: they can see an immediate improvement. If you don't organize one for conservation reasons, do one for the team-building effects.

Who: Contact members and volunteers. Also, contact the city sanitation department so they can pick up your filled trash bags when you're finished.

> *I do not recommend you organize a walkathon. They are very difficult to put together. Instead, gather some friends and walk as a group in an existing walkathon, and make sure the monies raised go to a charity whose philosophy you agree with.*

When: Invitations to the event should be sent at least three weeks ahead of time. RSVP if possible.

What: Bring gloves, trash bags, a first-aid kit, and plenty of bottled water.

• **WALKATHONS**. These are events where individuals receive donations from friends, coworkers, and neighbors for every mile they walk. All money raised is given to the charity organizing the event. For example, I stopped walking in the March of Dimes Walk America when I discovered that some of the money went to fund experiments on kittens, something I strongly oppose.

Who: Contact your friends, family, and members.

When: Contact everyone as soon as you receive information about the walkathon.

What: Be sure to register everyone for the event and distribute the pledge forms to them early so they, too, can collect pledges.

For the Intellectual

What do you think about? World politics? Chernobyl? Peace in the Middle East? Organize a special event to create a brainstorm of independent thoughts and ideas. Who knows? Maybe some Sunday afternoon you'll come up with a solution to world hunger.

- **WORKSHOPS**. Invite a specialist in your field of interest to present a workshop. Executives from non-profits, renowned change agents, and public relations consultants are great workshop speakers. These are terrific opportunities to train members how to make a difference. A college is a great place to host a workshop.

  Who: Ask a prominent expert in your field such as a local author or an elected official to present a talk. Check the local newspaper for human interest stories about people in your field; they might also be interested in being a presenter.

  When: Book a presenter three months ahead of time. Contact a local college or university as soon as possible about reserving a room. Send out notices two months ahead of time to ten times the number of people you can accommodate. For example, if you want fifty people to attend, send out five hundred invitations.

  What: Make sure you have enough people attending the workshop. If not, be smart and cancel the entire program out of respect for the presenter. Provide coffee and snack foods to keep people happy.

• **BOOK DISCUSSIONS**. On a cold Thursday night, a group of six people sit around a roaring fire sipping Blue Mountain Jamaican coffee, discussing a new political biography. Sound nice? Choose a topic-oriented book (the more controversial the better) to discuss with the interested members and the public. A bookstore is a great location for this event.

Who: Contact the manager of the bookstore to co-organize the event. The store might offer a special price on the chosen book to encourage people to purchase it. Post signs in the store inviting shoppers to attend the discussion.

When: Make your initial contact at least two months ahead of time.

What: Draw people to the discussion by offering free coffee, some snacks, and maybe a few door prizes. Send a news release to the local media, too. If the author lives nearby, send an invitation to him or her to attend and participate in the discussion.

• **SPEAKERS**. Inviting successful change agents and well-known personalities to speak to an audience is a great way to inspire people painlessly. Also, the general public can attend a presentation and not feel pressured to participate: it's a positive way to introduce people to new ideas. A college auditorium is a good place for a speech presentation.

Who: Contact the speaker or their assistant. For well-known presenters like Jane Goodall, you may need to place a booking at least a year ahead of time and pay an honorarium of up to $20,000. Too much? Try to get someone to do it for free, or if you have some funds, contact a speakers' bureau to place a booking for a less-expensive speaker. Often presenting an award to a speaker will encourage them to do the event gratis. Contact the college after booking the speaker.

When: Book a presenter three to five months ahead of time. Invite the public to attend by conducting a PR blitz. Send out news releases, do television appearances, conduct radio interviews, and post signs in high-traffic areas. The college communications office can also help with media relations. Do all of this at least two months ahead of time.

What: Make sure the speaker's miscellaneous arrangements are taken care of, like travel to and from the airport, housing, and meals.

- **LOBBY OUTINGS**. Take a trip to your state capitol or the U.S. Congress for a day of lobbying. By handling the travel and schedule for novice lobbyists, you can make their first lobbying experience fulfilling and easy.

  Who: Contact your members and interested nonmembers to determine how many people will be attending. Either reserve a bus or minivan through a travel agent (it'll cost from $100 to $500, depending on the size and traveling time) or organize a car pool among participants. If you decide to charter a bus, be sure the costs are evenly divided among the participants (e.g., $300 for the bus divided by thirty participants equals $10 apiece). Also schedule meetings with three legislators for that day.

  When: Contact your members at least a month ahead of time. Once you've figured out how many people are attending, make the final travel arrangements. Contact legislator's aides at least three weeks ahead of time.

  What: Make sure everyone dresses appropriately and is well informed about the legislative issues you'll be discussing.

- **ART SALE**. With a few bottles of wine, a free location, and a group of at least fifty people, you can host an art auction to benefit a good cause. There are companies who will set up this whole shebang: they bring the art, the auctioneer, people to process credit cards, even to serve the wine. You earn a royalty for every painting sold and keep every penny you make from ticket sales.

  Who: One good art auction fundraising company is Avatar Galleries. They have conducted art auctions for thousands of organizations, including the American Red Cross and the Children's Miracle Network. You can learn more about them at **www.avatargalleries.com**. You can also contact local galleries in your community to put together a similar event. You might even be able to obtain a higher royalty when you work with local businesses.

  When: Send invitations out at least two months ahead of time. Send public announcements to local newspapers and television stations a month before the auction. Contact the auction company as soon as you can, preferably six months before the event.

  What: Try to get a local wine store to donate a few cases of good wine for the event. Be sure to have some non-alcoholic beverages available, too.

- **ON-LINE AUCTION**. Technology has made our lives so much easier. If you're in a crunch for volunteers, hosting an on-line auction might be the way to go. Gather some unusual collectibles from supporters — artwork, antiques, signed memorabilia — and sell it on a reputable auction site. You can manage the whole process, monitor the auction activity, and ship out the items to the winning bidders. While this may not technically be an "event," it's a good example of how people are using the Internet to come together for the common good.

Who: Put the items up for bidding on reputable auction sites, such as Ebay (**www.ebay.com**) and Amazon Auctions (**auctions.amazon.com**). One company, **MissionFish.com**, brings buyers, donors, and non-profits together in a single marketplace by allowing charities to auction donated goods. Once you gather your items together, use a digital camera to photograph the items, write a catchy description, and explain that all the proceeds are going to charity.

When: Send out an e-mail to everyone to let them know about the auction. You may be surprised to learn that total strangers will also be bidding. Remember the motto, "One man's trash is another man's treasure."

What: The more unusual the items, the better. If someone can donate pieces with real value — jewelry or musical instruments, for example — then you're likely to generate a heated auction that nets lots of money for your cause.

School Events

Schools, being strapped for cash, are always appreciative of help from campus or community-based groups. Your show of generosity is an opportunity to influence, educate, and enlighten the minds of the citizens of tomorrow. These events are great for parental participation, too. Here are some of my favorites.

- **ASSEMBLIES**. Bring in interesting speakers, touring groups, or educational movies for the student body. You can ask the director of education of a like-minded national organization for a list of suggestions. But remember this tip in planning: the program should be tailored to the audience comprehension level (e.g., a screening of *Schindler's List* for a third-grade class is probably not appropriate).

Who: Contact the student council advisor or the high school principal. Also, contact the person in charge of booking your presenter.

When: Make your initial contact with the school at least a month before the start of the new school year so as to be included in that year's schedule. Book the presenter immediately after receiving approval from the school.

What: Be sure to have information — promotional fliers, press kits, and background information about your assembly — to present to the school. And do not charge the school for the assembly; they don't have the funds.

- **CONTESTS**. Who doesn't love a good competition? Organize a poster or essay contest focused around your cause. Offer a small prize — a trophy or gift certificate — for the winning entry. Be sure to send out a news release to the local newspaper to recognize the winner and other competitors. This is a great event for young kids.

  Who: Contact the school's principal. Ask him or her to spread the word about the contest through the school mail system and over the public address system.

  When: Make the initial contact at least a month before the start of the competition.

  What: Be specific on the theme of the contest. For example, instead of using "the environment" as a theme, consider something like "the endangered Florida Everglades." The less confusion the better.

- **DANCES**. Offer to sponsor the next school dance. Since the dance is already a regular weekly or monthly event, you don't need to market the dance or book the school's gym; it's already done. The dance's theme should reflect your cause (e.g., call it A Night in the Rainforest: you can decorate the event location using a tropical theme).

Provide plenty of literature and posters to accent the theme.

Who: Contact the dance coordinator, usually the student government advisor.

When: Contact the coordinator at least two months prior to your target date.

What: Be clear about your theme from the start. Also, consider placing a donation jar at the entrance for students to give a few dollars to a charity connected with the theme.

- **FIELD TRIPS**. Invite a class to take an educational outing. State parks, farms, food factories, and power plants are a few places kids enjoy visiting. Because youngsters have short attention spans, try to choose a place that teaches kids about your cause while entertaining them.

  Who: Contact the classroom teacher. Upon agreement, the teacher can handle the permission forms and paperwork to clear the trip with the school and parents.

  When: Contact the teacher at least three months prior to your ideal field trip date. Be sure to consider the weather. Don't plan a field trip during the winter months; it might snow.

  What: Make absolutely sure you have permission from the property owners or managers to bring a group of kids to your field trip site. Get it in writing. Also, make sure the teacher remembers to order a bus for that day.

- **HANDS-ON PROJECTS**. Great for younger kids. Co-organize with older students to educate students in grades K through 5 about your issue. High school students could discuss the benefit of living a drug-free lifestyle by serving as role models for these younger kids. Use arts and craft supplies to make it a truly hands-on project. Be creative and make it fun.

Who: Contact the teacher or school principal.

When: Make the initial contact at least two months prior to the desired date.

What: Provide all of the supplies and materials. If you need photocopies, make them ahead of time. Come prepared; the teacher will thank you.

Fund-Raising At Special Events

Any of the above fund-raising ideas can be used in conjunction with any of the above special events. I do not, however, recommend incorporating fund-raising into a school event. That would be tacky.

- **PLEDGE CARDS**. Leave pledge cards — an index-sized card that allows people to pledge a donation to your group — around the event site. They will encourage people to commit a small amount to your organization. Potential funds raised: $100 to $300.

- **ATTENDANCE FEES**. Leave a donation box at the entrance to the workshop or speaker's presentation for people to leave a contribution. Suggest a $1 to $3 freewill donation. If people feel uncomfortable donating, they don't have to. Potential funds raised: $100 to $500.

- **DONATION BOX**. Leave a donation jar by the refreshments table. When people help themselves to coffee and doughnuts, they're likely to leave a donation just because it's the courteous thing to do. Potential funds raised: $50 to $100.

• **RAFFLE.** Sell tickets during the event to raffle off a prize donated by a local business. Airline tickets, electronics, and gift baskets are great prizes. Sell individual tickets for $2, $3, and $5. Pick the winner at the end of the event. Potential funds raised: $100 to $600.

• **SELL BOOKS.** If the speaker is an author, purchase copies of the books in bulk from the publisher. Sell the autographed copies at the cover price to the audience. I found this is a great idea during the holiday season, almost a guaranteed sellout! Potential funds raised: $100 to $400.

After It's Over

Conduct a survey at the conclusion of your event to determine participants' overall satisfaction level. It is critical that you receive feedback. These opinions can be used to improve future events.

Randomly choose a few participants to fill out surveys on which you ask for general ideas and input. Also, ask for their ratings on specific aspects. For example, a good question for a workshop might be: On a scale of 1–10 (1 being the worst, 10 being the best), how would you rate the question-and-answer session of the workshop?

While the concept of special events hasn't changed over the years, the notion that they're hard to put together has. They're not. Try organizing one, and remember: practice makes perfect.

If You Liked This Chapter, You'll Love:

• Register at **E-Vite.com**. This on-line invitation service is free, convenient, and amazingly simple to use. Instead of sending out paper invitations through the mail, you can invite people to a special event via e-mail. By clicking on a special link, guests can RSVP instantly to your special page on E-Vite's website. People can see who else is invited, who is attending, and who has declined.

- If you need people to call a phone number to hear updated information or to RSVP to a special event, you can save money by getting a free voicemail box at **onebox.com**. This service will give you a local phone number in your community with a four-digit extension code. It works just like a regular voice mail service, except that it's free. Go to **onebox.com** and sign up today.

- Get a free fax number. **Efax.com** will assign you a private fax number where you can receive faxes. The faxes are directly routed, via a scanned image, to any e-mail account of your choosing. When you receive an e-fax, you can download it onto your PC for viewing; this is a great way to save important faxes digitally. Learn more about it at **www.efax.com**.

7

big business, big change:

Working with Companies

*"I find it rather easy to portray a businessman.
Being bland, rather cruel, and incompetent
comes naturally to me."*

John Cleese

WHEN I was a teenager, I was anti-Corporate America. I considered any company — technological, medical, retail — to be the enemy and it was my job to bring them down. I've grown up and realized the error of my ways. Yes, there are lots of conglomerates that must be held accountable for their actions, and I'm certainly in favor of not supporting them with my money. But there are also companies out there that are truly blending commerce with compassion, giving millions of dollars away to benefit the communities in which they serve or doing business in a socially-responsible manner.

Not Wild About Fur

When I was growing up in Reading, PA, I worked at the Reading Outlet Center, a discount retail area in town where a lot of my peers also worked. One year, I worked at Eddie Bauer, a retailer of outdoor and casual clothing for men and women. Because it was an outlet store, the stock was never regular — winter garments were often sold in the summer and summer clothing sold in the winter. One hot, humid day, a shipment of jackets arrived at the store. It was my job to unpack the jackets, hang them, and put them out on the sales floor. To my dismay, one of the large boxes contained heavy winter jackets trimmed with genuine coyote fur.

I've never been much of a supporter of throwing red paint or getting arrested for the sake of a cause. In this era of speedy technology and consumer clout, I knew there were better ways to express my angst about the jackets. So instead of screaming and yelling, I simply resigned and went home for the day.

Whenever trying to reform a corporation, the first step is to contact the offending business. It's sad that so many times we assume a corporation is the enemy. There are many instances when a company simply doesn't know what they've done and will gladly change their ways once hearing your views. But in this case, Eddie Bauer (or the receptionist on the phone) was well aware of the fur usage and simply didn't care.

Step two. Using my network of members, I blasted an e-mail to over 25,000 teens, who in turn forwarded that e-mail to their friends and family. In just minutes, tens of thousands of people were asked not to purchase clothes from Eddie Bauer, to return merchandise to the store with a kind anti-fur letter, to e-mail and phone Eddie Bauer to lodge a complaint, and even to return Eddie Bauer catalogs (at the company's expense) with the message, "Return to sender: don't use fur."

In a few weeks, Eddie Bauer released a statement that, due to the lack of consumer interest in fur, the coyote fur would be replaced with wool. It really was that easy. And we did it by proving that consumers wanted a fur-free shopping environment.

They're Not All Bad

The lesson of that story is that many companies aren't even aware of the error of their ways. We like to imagine that corporations are these giant conglomerates with people in pinstripe suits sitting in large board rooms plotting how to take over the world. The reality is that people who run companies are just that: people. Companies run by good-hearted individuals generally give back to the communities in which they do business. And vice versa: corporations run by people with ill-intentions, usually are the ones we read about in the papers being picketed by protestors or disgruntled employees.

Right On Target

One company that is revolutionizing corporate philanthropy is Target. Target is the fourth largest discount retailer in the United States, known for their clever advertising campaign that romanticizes their logo, the red bull's eye.

So it seems natural that a retailer that prides itself for unusual juxtapositions would also do something unusual on the corporate-giving side. Instead of making one-time donations or small gestures to charities, Target gives a percentage of their sales to charities in the community in which they do business. They give up to one million dollars a week. Shoppers can even use their Target credit card to earmark which school in their town will receive a percentage of their purchase. The point: Target mixes commerce with philanthropy, believing that if they are not only a good retailer, but also a company that supports worthy causes in a big way, then people will be more inclined to shop there. Their soaring profits reflect that.

Whole Foods is another pioneer in corporate philanthropy. The upscale health food supermarket chain sells good-quality, wholesome foods. Because their buyers seek out the freshest produce and food free of preservatives and chemicals, it makes perfect sense that Whole Foods would take an active role in food safety issues.

Whole Foods actively participates in legislation on food issues that affect all of us — such as seafood sustainability, use of pesticides on produce, genetic engineering, and the pros and cons of irradiation of our food. They even make these often confusing scientific topics understandable through the use of informative fliers and promotional materials available throughout their store and website: **www.wholefoods.com**

One of the best things about Whole Foods is their commitment to community. Every month, each store — under the Whole Foods, Fresh Fields, and Bread & Circus names — gives away five percent of one day's total sales to charity. The local organization doesn't have to do anything to earn the money; they simply pick up a check at the end of the day. It's one of the better examples of corporate selflessness that their competitors should follow.

Finally, some companies are so generous that they don't generate any profits for themselves. Newman's Own is a specialty food manufacturer founded by actor Paul Newman that funds a number of humanitarian and conservation organizations all over the world. Their motto, "Shameless Exploitation in the Pursuit of the Common Good," reflects the company's donation of 100% of all profits to charity. When you buy a jar of Newman's Own popcorn or salad dressing, you can feel good knowing every penny went to a good cause.

Cause-Related Marketing

So why are companies like Target giving millions away to charity? Why not keep it in their coffers and fatten their bottom line? Well, that's exactly it. Some corporations believe in the spiritual philosophy, "What goes around, comes around." If they do good, they'll do a good business.

Carol Cone is the founder of Cone Communications, a marketing firm based in Boston, Massachusetts. I met Carol in 1999 when I teamed up with a digital divide advocacy group in New York City to help bring technology to kids who needed it most. She is credited with creating the concept of "cause-related marketing." Carol is famous for teaming up big-name corporations with good causes. For example, Carol helped create the Avon Breast Cancer Crusade, Reebok Human Rights Awards, Heinz Family Works, Kimberly-Clark Community Playgrounds Project, and Polaroid Kid's Care project.

What's so ingenious about Carol's pioneering approach to marketing is that corporations, especially brands in a competitive field, need to implement strategies that help differentiate them from their competitors. One good way is to tie corporations with causes. But instead of doing this in a small way — which could potentially backlash if the public perceives it as nothing more than a PR stunt — Cone advises her clients to do it right. And that's why many corporations who start these programs make it an integral part of the company that lasts for many years. When Avon commits to supporting breast cancer research, they're in it for the long run.

Making Changes

But companies will make bad decisions. And it's your decision whether to simply refuse to do business with them or to do it in a way that will probably generate the result you want: to inform them of your reasons in the clearest, most concise, and effective way possible.

The point is that despite the billions of dollars corporations have in their coffers, there is one thing that you have that they

> When I contacted
> Eddie Bauer,
> I realized that this retailer
> catered mainly to a
> young, urban audience.
> That's what made
> Eddie Bauer cool.
> And since I headed
> a national organization
> of teenagers
> from all over the country,
> I knew Eddie Bauer
> would listen to us.
> I found the angle,
> used it in a strong
> but not militant fashion,
> and got the result I wanted.

don't: consumer power. Without your purchases of basic household products, groceries, cars, clothing — you name it — there would be no company. In other words, your opinions really do count.

But how can one person's decision not to purchase Brand A make a company change? Well, it won't. But if thousands of people decide to switch purchases, it's often enough to make a company notice. Sure, it won't affect their bottom line, but it's a ripple that, given the right opportunity, could become a typhoon of a problem. These companies would prefer to deal with the situation now, rather than dealing with a real monster down the road.

I believe the most powerful tools we have are the power to vote and the ability to decide which goods and services to purchase. With so many corporations in competition for your money, you have the capability to speak up against corporate abuse by refusing to patronize a particular business. No matter how many commercials, celebrity spokespeople, and free samples a corporation may tempt you with, they shouldn't receive a dime from you if you disagree with their policies. With more and more consumers refusing to purchase certain brands or products in hopes of effecting some corporate change, shopping with a conscience is becoming a popular way for individuals to express their views.

When others see people taking action against a corporation, they'll want to take a stand, too. It is, after all, simply an organized method of communicating complaints to the company. Corporations aren't in the business of generating bad press or ill-will from their consumer base; they want to do everything possible to meet your needs and often will change their ways when asked to.

Voting with Your Money

Groups of citizens launch campaigns against corporations for a variety of reasons. Environmentalists ran a campaign against Mitsubishi, a Japanese conglomerate, for their rainforest clearcutting practices. Morality groups refused to shop at a chain of bookstores because they carried material the group deemed "morally offensive." This is a silent, yet effective way, to voice your opinion with a strong dose of "and I mean it!" When people are upset over a corporation's policy or action, they usually attract media attention and their actions educate the public about an issue that might otherwise get ignored.

Does it Really Work?

Back in the 1980s, consumers and animal lovers were up in arms that the cosmetics industry still tested their lotions, potions, and creams on animals. We saw those horrific photos of rabbits having various solutions poured into their eyes. Even people in the scientific community, who experiment on animals for medical reasons, were sympathetic to the cause.

So an organization put together a list of cosmetics companies that promised not to test their products on animals. Many of these manufacturers were small, family-owned companies that sold only in specialty stores and boutiques. But consumers purchased these items in droves, making a conscious choice to buy these products. It didn't matter how much more they cost. And companies that didn't make the list? They were singled out for being cruel and disgusting, words a marketing executive wouldn't want associated with a beauty company.

Because so many consumers demanded that their toiletries and cosmetics not be tested on animals, the beauty industry decided to turn this public relations lemon into lemonade. They invented "cruelty-free" products for this new market of conscious consumers. For example, The Body Shop's slogan "Against Animal Testing," can be seen boldly printed on their products, on giant signs in the stores, and on T-shirts worn by company employees. The Body Shop did the right thing and made millions of dollars reaping the benefits of being the "good guy" in the industry. Today, very few cosmetic corporations want the negative image that comes with animal testing.

This is a fantastic example of how consumers can be educated, holding an entire industry accountable for their actions. In the beginning, the few visionaries who spoke up were considered "kooks." But in the end, millions of animals were spared and the industry reformed as a result of consumer action.

How do I Start?

You read in the morning newspaper that the town's largest employer has decided to eliminate health benefits for their workers. Your neighbors, Mary and John, have a six-year-old child who needs those benefits because she suffers from a terminal illness. You read further and discover that the company will save only a few thousand dollars by cutting the program. You want to help.

Before launching an all-out campaign effort, try to bring attention single-handedly to the cause. Sometimes even one person can force a company to change. When I was thirteen years old, I was upset to see a live lobster being thrown onto the floor and smashed to pieces on the TV game show "Supermarket Sweep." I wrote a letter to the producer of the show, telling him to remove the live lobsters or I would stop watching the show. In a few days, the producer agreed to my request. I won! I didn't have to spend more than the price of a stamp on the effort.

But if your phone call to the company goes nowhere, it's time to group some people together and get your opinions heard loud and clear.

Your First Steps

Find out the name of the chief executive officer or chairman of the corporation. Also, get the mailing address of the corporate headquarters where the decision-making executives work.

One of the easiest things, and perhaps most effective, is to send an e-mail directed to the right person. The funny thing about e-mail is that even though it's impersonal, we all retrieve it in the same way. Unlike mail, which can get routed to a desk or, worse, the trash can, e-mail usually ends up popping up directly on the recipient's computer screen. When you e-mail the CEO of a corporation, there's a good chance that he or she will actually read it — and might even reply right away.

Of course, they also have the option of ignoring it outright. And that's a reality you'll have to accept. But your e-mail at least gets read, and it could be the seed that germinates change at the company.

Okay, so you're wondering how you obtain their e-mail address. Simple: because most corporations value the speed and efficiency of e-mail, they usually require that everyone, including upper management, have e-mail addresses that are the same format as everyone else's. So if Bob Smith in accounting's email is bobsmith@yourcompany.com then it's a good chance the CEO, Carol Walker, would probably be **carolwalker@yourcompany. com**. And if not, your message will just get sent back to you.

According to **planetfeedback.com**, an on-line portal that helps consumers express their satisfaction or dissatisfaction to a corporation, it's important to give details when sending your opinion and to end with a course of action. In other words, tell them what's wrong and what they can do to fix the problem. It's also critical that you provide your contact information so a representative from the company can communicate with you. If you received an anonymous letter, would you take it seriously?

If you can't locate the e-mail address, consider handwriting a letter. Type or neatly hand write a one-page letter to the CEO or chairman explaining that you are a devoted customer and feel their plans are inappropriate. In the instance of the corporation cutting benefits to employees, explain how the elimination of benefits will hurt the workers, perhaps giving first-hand examples of the children and family members who so desperately need the coverage. Be specific — never, ever vulgar! — in your letter. It's also a good idea to send the letter via certified mail to make sure that they receive it.

> *It's important to follow up on your letter. Call, write, fax. If you can, try to set up a meeting with the CEO of the company so you can further express your concerns face-to-face.*

The smaller the company, the more realistic it is that a meeting could happen. The more you follow-up, the more the company will realize how serious and committed you are. It's really a test of perseverance here.

Other Ways to Get Heard

Because there is so much competition among similar corporations, many businesses offer toll-free and postage-paid outlets for consumers to offer suggestions on how the corporation can improve its goods and services. It's called relationship marketing. You can express your opinions at *their* expense. It's okay to take advantage of these opportunities; in fact, many corporations rely on consumer feedback to guide the direction of the company. Some of these outlets include:

• **800 COMMENT LINES**. Call 1 (800) 555•1212 (toll-free) and ask the operator if the corporation has an 800 phone number. Look on the back of packages, in catalogs, on websites, on promotional fliers — on anything produced by the company. The funny thing about these toll-free numbers is that

> *Many businesses offer toll-free and postage-paid outlets for consumers to offer suggestions on how the corporation can improve its goods and services. It's called relationship marketing. You can express your opinions at their expense.*

corporations set them up so you *will* call. The corporation pays: it's free for you to call as many times as you like. Have others call too to share their thoughts.

• **COMMENT CARDS**. Many retail stores have postage-paid comment cards dispersed throughout their stores for shoppers to use to evaluate the store's goods and services. You can fill them out and mail them — no postage necessary! The corporation pays a high premium to the postal service for the business-reply service. There is no limit to the number of cards you can fill out: they are, after all, free. I once filled out a card thanking the store for not selling fur; I received a real letter from the company expressing their appreciation for the compliment.

• **CATALOGS**. If you receive a catalog from a boycotted company, send it back at the company's expense. Write "return to sender" and circle on the return address. Be sure to leave your comments on the catalog cover for them to read. The company pays for postage; you get your message heard.

• **WEBSITE**. Post your views, action alerts, and updates on the company's website. Lots of business-to-consumer websites (**amazon.com**, for example, is a b-c) have sections where people can direct their comments to the right department. These e-mails do get read.

You can also visit message boards at some sites. At television network websites, message boards are usually visited by people who want to gossip or chat about television programming. But some people share ideas and make comments on serious issues. Believe it or not, these boards are monitored by people at the network who report to management on unusual trends found there. Even talk show host Rosie O'Donnell has been known to read messages on her official website; you never know who's on-line.

Teaming Up With A Corporate Partner

Target's innovative program   gives a percentage of shopper's purchases to a specific school the shopper indicates they'd like to support. More than 104,000 K-12 schools across the United States participate. Any public, private, parochial, or tax-exempt educational institution can participate. And they've even set-up a toll-free number people can call if they have questions or want to sign up. (That number, by the way, is **1 (800) 316•6142**.)

This is just one good example of how corporations, more than ever, are making it easier for you to team up with them on worthy causes in your community. Your brother doesn't have to be the president of the company for you to get an "in;" on the contrary, you can find an ally based solely on the merits of your work.

Some other good examples:

• Clothing retailer The Gap has authorized every Gap retail outlet to give away gift certificates and t-shirts to local organizations working with young people, the arts, or the environment. Local groups simply need to contact the store's manager, fill out a brief application, and wait for approval. I've done it lots of times with no hassle whatsoever.

- Nike builds playgrounds, sports surfaces, and soccer fields all over the world as part of their reuse-a-shoe program. Old sneakers — any brand — are collected and ground down into tiny pieces. The shock-absorbent material is used to make sports surfaces which are installed in communities where kids don't have places to play. You can learn more at **www.nikebiz.com**. Maybe you can get one built in your town.

- Ikea, the global lifestyle furniture retailer, is always donating furnishings and accessories to local organizations. In the United Kingdom, they donated 200,000 cans of paint to local hospitals, schools, and non-profit groups.

While you may not team up with a corporation to host a fashion benefit party (Victoria's Secret hosted one in Cannes, France, that benefited AmFar, the AIDS organization, and netted well over two million dollars), you can definitely take advantage of their programs at the local level.

So once you determine what you need, then you need to figure out who carries the product. Do you want sneakers for kids at a local school who

> *The first thing you need to do*
> *is figure out*
> *what exactly you need.*
> *Remember, just because*
> *something is free*
> *doesn't mean you need it.*
> *Why invest all your time*
> *in obtaining 500 free t-shirts*
> *if you don't have*
> *a plan of action*
> *to use them*
> *to benefit charity?*

otherwise can't afford athletic apparel for gym class? Perhaps a local footwear distributor, like Footlocker, could help you approach Nike or Reebok for shoes. Do you want to have a bake sale? Ask for free cookies, breads, and cakes from local bakeries. You'd be surprised how generous or helpful people can be if you ask on behalf of a good cause.

Another good idea is to take a cue from Carol Cone: create a co-branding opportunity. When a new business is opening shop in your town, or a company is launching a new product, tie your group in with them. When I was helping a digital divide advocacy group raise money to buy computers for kids, we teamed up with a computer parts manufacturer. When they launched their new monitor, they gave $50 to the group for every new product sold that month. Because the money went to a good cause, people were more inclined to buy their monitor instead of a competitor's. It's a win-win situation!

Not Free Trade

A phrase you might hear, but not know too much about, is fair trade. The concept was brought to the masses by cosmetics giant The Body Shop in their "Trade, Not Aid" line of products. In short, fair trade is a company's efforts to pay a real wage to producers in Asia, Africa, Latin America and other parts of the world for their materials, labor, or finished products.

Shopping in the Fair Trade Market

According to the Fair Trade Federation (**www.fairtradefederation. com**), fair trade means "an equitable and fair partnership between marketers and producers" by which people living and working outside of North America are given the same opportunity North Americans have to make a decent living. "A fair trade partnership works to provide low-income artisans and farmers with a living wage for their work." Some of the criteria include:

• Paying a fair wage in the local context.
• Offering employees opportunities for advancement.
• Providing equal employment opportunities for all people, particularly the most disadvantaged.
• Engaging in environmentally sustainable practices.
• Being open to public accountability.
• Building long-term trade relationships.
• Providing healthy and safe working conditions within the local context.
• Providing financial and technical assistance to producers whenever possible.

While it's nearly impossible to buy products that are fair trade-approved for everything you need, I think it's important that we support companies that provide fair trade products. If you need hand lotion, for example, take the extra step to buy The Body Shop cocoa lotion; since 1993, The Body Shop has been paying the premium price for cocoa beans — thus helping poor communities all over the world to thrive a bit better.

In Summation

We shouldn't lump corporations into one giant group and assume they are all bad. Granted, there are some corrupt companies that need to be opposed, but we must also make time to thank those corporate leaders who are doing the right thing. When a company gives millions to charity, take a few minutes to drop a postcard in the mail expressing your appreciation for their generosity. Remember: a kind word goes a long way.

Most importantly, it's up to us, the consumers, to make wise and intelligent choices in our shopping. Every time we buy something, we cast important "votes" in favor of corporations who do business in a socially responsible manner. It is our responsibility to become an educated consumer, to shop wisely, and to voice our opinions when something bad happens.

If You Liked This Chapter, You'll Love:

- Read *Shopping for a Better World* by the Council on Economic Priorities (New York: Ballantine, 1993). It grades popular consumer goods on issues ranging from environmental protection to women's issues. While many of the reports are now outdated, it's still a good primer to learn how far cause-related commerce has come since the early 90s.

- Join the Center for the Study of Commercialism (CSC). This national organization works to encourage people to spend more time together doing constructive activities instead of becoming a nation of couch potatoes. Write: **CSC, 1875 Connecticut Avenue, NW, Suite 300, Washington, DC 20009-5728**.

- The Internet has provided us with some websites that make our lives so much easier. One of those sites is **www.planetfeedback.com**. On this website, you can send letters of praise or dissent to a number of big-name companies. They'll forward the letter to the appropriate person via e-mail, or if the CEO doesn't have a known e-mail account, they'll fax or mail it for free. You can monitor, track, and read other letters, too.

- The Natural Step (TNS) is a non-profit environmental group working to "build an ecologically and economically sustainable society." Working with leaders in the business, academic, and government communities, their goal is to redesign their activities to achieve a greener planet. Big-name companies like Nike and Ikea are on-board. Learn more at **www.naturalstep.org**, or check out the book *The Natural Step for Business: Wealth, Ecology, and the Evolutionary Corporation*, by Brian Nattrass and Mary Altomare (New Society Publishers, 1999).

8

the single crusader:

One Person Really Can Make a Difference

*"I may climb perhaps to no great heights,
but I will climb alone."*

Cyrano De Bergerac

IF you've gotten this far into the book and thought to yourself, "Where can I find the time to make a difference?" then this chapter is for you. Today, time is a real precious commodity. All of us try to cram as much as possible into our day. But for some reason, most of us never get around to contributing something worthy to our community.

The good news is that making a difference doesn't have to be time-consuming or even labor intensive. In fact, you can do it all by yourself. There's really no need to start a group, launch a campaign, or organize anything.

> *Just find a few minutes in your day and do something simple, yet concrete, to change the world.*

In my book *Heaven on Earth:15-Minute Miracles to Change the World*, I write how you can help someone in need or make your community a healthier place to live — in less than fifteen-minutes a day. These are not just random acts of kindness. I'm actually not fond of random acts of kindness because they require only that you be nice to someone, and while this is a kind gesture, it's not an act of service. Instead, my philosophy is to take advantage of technology, maximize your available time, and achieve a specific result in just a few minutes flat.

Working The Media

Even without an organization behind you, you can get your opinion heard. The best way to start is with the three media outlets: television, radio, and print. You won't be writing news releases or creating press kits in your one-person campaign. Instead, you'll be commenting on erroneous stories or features, and in the process keeping out-of-line journalists and producers in line with your views.

Newspapers

Write a letter to the editor as often as you can. If you disagree with an editorial or news article written in the newspaper, let the editor and readership know about it. Writing a letter to the editor is easy. Letters should be brief (two hundred words) and address a specific topic of general public concern or interest. For verification purposes, include your full name, address, and telephone number. Concise letters will get preferential treatment. Check your newspaper for specific guidelines and an address or e-mail to send your letter to.

If you have good letter writing skills, contact the editor of a small newspaper and offer to write a weekly, biweekly, or monthly column for their publication *free of charge*. Small newspapers are usually struggling financially, so your offer to write for them gratis might be eagerly accepted. Who knows? Maybe your free writing will turn into a full-time, salaried job by the end of the year. Stranger things have happened.

Magazines

Reach a national audience by sending a letter to your favorite magazine. If you disagree with comments made in the magazine, send a letter explaining why you oppose those views. Or, if you agree with a controversial article, send a letter of support for that point of view. If you don't think your letter will get published, send it anyway. Lots of magazine editors review these letters to get a sense how their readership is reacting to the magazine. While your letter may not get published, it can influence future articles, content, and even the overall direction of the publication.

Television

Contact national television networks when a show does or promotes something you deem offensive. Address your letter to "The Office of the President." For example, if you believe a kids' show is too violent, write to the network and express your feelings. You can keep up-to-date on the comings and goings of the entertainment industry by reading *Variety* magazine on-line daily at **www.variety.com** and learn everything about the media industry at **www.inside.com**. These two websites are bookmarked on my browser. For cable networks, go on-line to their respective websites and find out how to send your comments.

Radio

Call a radio talk show to express your views, opposing or supporting the show's guests. If you do it during your morning and evening commute via cell phone, be sure you're not breaking any cell-phone usage laws in your community. Even though I advised against using a cell phone when you are the guest being interviewed, this is different; you're a listener in this case, calling in with a comment.

Smaller stations also let listeners produce and host their own radio program. It works like public access television: you host a regularly-scheduled program on a topic of your choice. While the market may be much smaller than, say, a Howard Stern program, you're still reaching a group of people. The great thing about radio is that you can pre-tape lots of shows, so if you're free for a few days, you can tape a few weeks' worth of shows in advance.

Polls

Participate in polls offered by your local newspaper or television nightly news show. Surprisingly, many legislators check these polls to get a general feel as to how their constituents feel about certain issues. Television news and website polls are read and monitored by influential people, so getting your voice heard is really important.

Taking Financial Stock

When I began investing in the stock market a few years ago, I made it a point to put my money only into companies that followed my criteria: that they be socially-responsible as well as profitable.

The way you handle your financial transactions and investments can have a profound impact on our world. By taking a few extra steps to put your money in the right places, you can not only build a nest egg for yourself, but actually help non-profit groups raise money. Talk about multi-tasking! Check out these options:

Conscious Checks

Order specialty checks that benefit your favorite organization instead of buying checks from the bank. These checks support the work of organizations like the Sierra Club, Greenpeace, and the

National Organization for Women. For free information, contact Message! Products toll-free at **1 (800) 243•2565** or write them at **P.O. Box 64800, St. Paul, MN 55164-0800** or visit their website: **www.greenmoney.com/message**

Socially Responsible Investing

Choose a mutual fund that invests not only in profitable businesses but also in business promoting positive social change. Here are some sample firms (not necessarily an endorsement):

- *Calvert Group.* Founded in 1982, Calvert Group is the creator of the first environmentally and socially responsible funds. Call **1 (800) 368•2748** for a free prospectus or visit their website: **www.calvertgroup.com**

- *Pax World Fund.* This is a no-load, diversified mutual fund that invests only in industries involved in pollution control, health care, and education. They do not invest in weapons, tobacco, alcohol, or gambling industries. Call **1 (800) 767•1729** for a free prospectus or write **224 State Street, Portsmouth, NH 03801**, or contact their website at **www.paxfund.com**.

- *Ethical Funds.* The slogan of Canada's leading socially-responsible investment firm is is 'Do the Right Thing.' They offer the largest selection of carefully screened mutual funds that are socially and environmentally friendly. Visit **www.ethicalfunds.com** to learn more.

Also, ask your broker if his or her company already has a socially-responsible fund. Lots of investment firms now have funds that avoid tobacco stocks, guns and gun-related companies, and widely-known environmental offenders.

For general information about socially responsible investing, contact *The Greenmoney Journal*, a newsletter covering the latest in socially responsible investing and business. Write **P.O. Box 67, Santa Fe, NM 87504**; or check out their website: **www.greenmoney.com**

A good primer on investing with compassion is *Investing with Your Values: Making Money and Making a Difference*, by Hal Brill, Jack A. Brill and Cliff Feigen-baum, (New Society Publishers, 2000). If you want to get your feet wet on socially-responsible investing, this a great place to start.

> *When choosing a fund, make sure the person managing your money is not just socially responsible but also a whiz at picking stocks. Look at the fund's performance over the last three years and see if it beat the NASDAQ average.*

Plastic with Purpose

Every time you use an affinity credit card, a portion of your purchase (around ten cents) goes to support non-profit groups like Family Violence Prevention Fund; a flat donation per purchase is made to the designated charity. For free information about the affinity cards of Mastercard and Visa, contact Working Assets at **1 (800) 788•8588**, or if possible, sign up for a card from your favorite national association.

Lots of national organizations also offer their own affinity card. Some examples:

- American Association of Retired Persons (AARP). If you're retired, this card is perfect for you.
- Elton John AIDS Foundation Visa. With every purchase you make, a percentage is given to the charity.
- National Wildlife Federation (NWF) Visa. The NWF receives three dollars when you sign up.

These cards, and many others, can be applied for on-line at **www.creditcardcatalog.com/ affinity**

Buy Right

Instead of hitting the mall during the holiday season, shop for gifts from catalogs and stores run by non-profit organizations. Purchase calendars, T-shirts, coffee mugs, books, and other items that benefit a worthy charity. A portion of each sale will go directly to support the designated group's work.

Before you sign up for a card, make sure that a donation will be made to a specific charity. Many credit cards look like they support a charity but actually don't. For example, a credit card with a picture of a forest on it does not necessarily give any funds to an environmental group. Do your homework.

The merchandise may even be exclusive to the charity. A few years ago, designer Todd Oldham created stylish winter hats to benefit an animal protection group. Not only did all of the proceeds benefit a good cause, but the hats were also a very chic gift.

A website I like to shop at is ShopforChange. Every time you buy merchandise from one of the popular retailers at ShopforChange, they donate five percent of your purchase price to a variety of humanitarian and civic non-profit groups. The donation is automatic, at no cost to the consumer, as long as you access the merchants through their site. Visit **www.shopforchange .com**.

Armchair Lobbying

Don't have time to meet with your legislators? Not a problem. Don't even have time to write a personal letter to your legislator? Not a problem. It's easy to keep in touch with your elected officials – all from the comfort of your home.

Purchase one hundred postage-paid postcards from the post office and keep them handy. Whenever you see a news story

> You can find out the names of your federal representative and two federal senators by contacting your local League of Women Voters. Also, the League can give you the names and addresses of your local and state elected officials. Check the blue pages in your phone book for your town's local LWV chapter. In Canada, you can log onto *www.canadaonline.about.com* for a truly comprehensive listing of Canadaian government and consumer resources.

about pending legislation or an issue facing your community, you can quickly dash off a comment to your elected officials right away. So many times, we read or see something and think, "I should probably do something." But we soon forget and our congressman never hears from us. This way, you don't have an excuse. And be sure to drop a note once in a while when your elected official does something you approve of. They receive letters expressing discontent much more often than praise, so your note is sure to stick out and be read.

Join a National Organization's Action Network

Many groups, including the Humane Society of the United States and Children's Defense Fund have a network which alerts its active members to pending legislation at all levels of government that needs letters of support or opposition. It's armchair lobbying made easy.

Switch Phone Carriers

Working Assets Long-Distance Service gives a percentage of your monthly phone bill to groups that help people, clean up our environment, and more. But they also update you on key legislative bills in Congress on your monthly phone statement. They even foot the bill for your call to Washington. For information, visit their website at **www.wald.com**

Attend a Hearing

Contact your state legislator to obtain permission to attend a legislative hearing at your state capitol. See government in action and learn a few things about civics. You'll be surprised how interesting the hearings are. Bring a friend. Once you familiarize yourself with how these meetings are run, you can comment at your local government hearings and possibly be inspired to run for office down the road.

Vote

Your vote counts at all levels of government. It's your responsibility, not just your right, to vote. Rock the Vote can help: they were founded by members of the recording industry in 1990 in response to a wave of attacks on freedom of speech and artistic expression. To register to vote, call **1 (800) 249•VOTE** or check out Rock the Vote's website: **www.rockthevote.org**

"Suppose You had $20"

Instead of spending twenty bucks to buy a pair of "slightly damaged" denim jeans from the Gap, use it to do good. By using your money to help a non-profit group, enlighten a young mind, or educate an elected official, you're making a bigger impact than you might think. Here are some ways to spend a few dollars to do just that:

• **DONATE A SUBSCRIPTION.** Pick your favorite topic-oriented magazine (e.g., *Audubon* for conservation) and donate a year's subscription to the local public or high school library.

- **BUY BULK BOOKS**. Purchase a few copies of a book on your favorite topic and send one each to your state representative and senator. Your book will educate them about your interest and, in essence, lobby them on future legislation. And yes, I will make a plug for my own book: purchase copies of this book and distribute them to local high school libraries to teach a young person how to make a difference.

- **DISTRIBUTE VIDEOS**. Many national organizations sell professionally produced videos about their work and campaigns. Order copies of your favorites and give them to public libraries and video stores for their community-service section. The public can rent these movies free of charge.

- **RENEW YOUR MEMBERSHIP**. National organizations depend heavily on membership dues for income; to some groups, dues represent 90 percent of their funding. Be sure to pay your basic dues every year. If you're worried about receiving annoying mailings throughout the year, request that your name not be brokered to other organizations or businesses. Another reason to renew: if your favorite organization is a 501(c) 3 organization, your contribution is tax deductible.

- **GIFT MEMBERSHIPS**. Buy your friend or legislator a year's membership in your favorite national group. They'll receive the publications and materials year round, keeping them informed of issues you care about. Remember to make clear on the membership form the individual who is receiving the new membership and that you're the one paying the dues.

On A Spare Saturday Morning

No matter how busy you think your life is, sooner or later you will have a spare weekday or weekend to devote some time to a project. But what to do? You can't just pick up a paint brush and start painting over graffiti.

First, contact local non-profit groups to see if there are organized volunteer days you can be a part of. If not, give these a try:

- VolunteerMatch utilizes the power of the Internet to help individuals nationwide find volunteer opportunities posted by local non-profit and public sector organizations. Visit **www.volunteermatch.org** to learn more.

- In Canada, Volunteer Canada is the national voice for volunteerism in Canada. Since 1977, Volunteer Canada has been committed to supporting volunteerism and civic participation through ongoing programs and special projects. Visit **www.volunteer.ca**

- Founded in 1990, the Points of Light Foundation is a non-partisan, non-profit organization devoted to promoting volunteerism. With a network of over 500 volunteer centers, you're sure to find a project right in your own backyard. Go on-line at **www.pointsoflight.org**

If all fails, here are some good projects that you can do by yourself or with the help of a friend. Give them a try and have a productive Saturday afternoon:

Make a Library Display

Ask the librarian at your local public library for permission to set up a display about your issue. For example, if your main issue of concern is conservation, you can create a display using pamphlets, facts, and charts from the Nature Conservancy, as well as a listing of local support groups.

Make a Vertical File

Gather news clippings, photographs, pamphlets, charts, graphs, and posters about your cause for a special vertical file for your library. These files cover general topics from homelessness to AIDS prevention and are used by students for research projects. Be sure to ask the librarian for permission first.

Get a Political Life

Help out a candidate you support by volunteering for his or her campaign. On a weekend morning, your duties may include posting signs around town, working the phones, or stuffing envelopes for a mass mailing. Your help will make a big difference in their campaign. Contact the local committee of the party of your choice for information on how you can help.

Thank Someone

Write several thank-you letters to legislators or corporations for doing the right thing. Rarely do they receive kind letters for doing good deeds. Your doing so will encourage them to continue their streak of goodness.

Volunteer

Spend a few hours helping out at a local community non-profit center. Walk the dogs at the animal shelter. Help cook lunch at the church soup kitchen. Create a database program at a local AIDS hospice. Do your part.

What You Can Do in One Minute

That busy, huh? There are several small things you can do to express your opinions, and they all take less than one minute. Don't disappoint me by making these actions the only things you do for our planet; add them to other ideas and skills addressed in the book.

- **GO ON-LINE.** More and more websites are popping up that raise money for charity with the simple click of the mouse. Go on-line at **www.thehungersite.com** and **www.therainforestsite .com** to donate food and preserve rainforest land. By clicking on a button, you'll be directed to a page of advertisements that pay for your automatic donation. Visit daily to do your part.

- **SAVE SOUP LABELS.** The Campbell Soup Company has been running their Labels for Education program for years to benefit schools. It's simple to participate: just peel off the label from a Campbell Soup can and give a small bundle of them to a local school. They redeem them for points that can be used to purchase educational tools like iMac computers and art supplies. Learn more at **www.labelsforeducation.com**.

- **POINT OF PURCHASE.** At the register at the grocery store, many grocers are now allowing you to make an automatic donation at the register to fight hunger in your community. You can donate one to five dollars, with all of the proceeds benefiting a local food bank. With all those savings from double coupon day, why not give some of it back?

- **GIVE USED EYEWEAR.** The next time you get your eyeglasses replaced, don't take your old glasses home with you. Many national chain eye centers have drop-off boxes for used glasses; they'll refit them and give them to people in Third World countries to correct their visual impairments free of charge.

- **DONATE USED CELL PHONES**. If you get your current cell phone replaced, don't throw away the old one. The Wireless Foundation takes your old cell phones, reprograms them to dial 9-1-1 at the touch of a button, and gives them to domestic violence victims so they can call for support free of charge. Visit **donateaphone .com** to learn more.

If You Liked This Chapter, You'll Love:

- Check out my book *Heaven on Earth:15-Minute Miracles to Change the World*. It's chock-full of over 100 fifteen-minute miracles — simple ways to help in just minutes a day. I also write a daily column at **MyPotential.com**, a leading personal growth website which is home to leading spiritualists such as Deepak Chopra and the Dali Lama. The column that lists these clever ideas is called "Fast Philanthropy."

- Sign up for a daily e-newsletter at **lifeminders.com**. This content-rich, free e-mail service will send you current, up-to-date information on topics of your choice, including horoscopes, politics, and news. It's an easy way to stay informed.

- Make a list of simple fifteen-minute miracles and write each on a 3" x 5" card. Bundle a few together and give them to busy people who say, "I never have the time to make a difference." They'll appreciate knowing that they can call an airline to donate frequent flier miles or visit a website like **thehungersite.com** and give a little back right there on the spot.

9
awards:

Getting the Recognition You Deserve

"Winning is a habit.
Unfortunately, so is losing"

Vince Lombardi

I once read a *Businessweek* article that discussed the idea that anyone can become a brand. Branding is the process of taking a concept, a name, or a word and giving it a unique identity. What does Brand A stand for? What would Brand A do in this situation? What three words describe Brand A? These are just a few of the questions that people who "brand" themselves ask. People like Michael Graves, Martha Stewart, and even chef Emeril Lagasse have become personal brands.

Branding doesn't happen overnight. It takes time, a proven track record, and some really good PR. While this has been used in the corporate world for a long time, I've rarely seen it used for charitable purposes. And the reason is simple: people wonder, "Isn't it wrong to brand something affiliated with charity?" I don't think so. Just because a technique is so closely associated with the for-profit world doesn't make it unethical to use in the non-profit world.

The advantage of branding acts of service is that once the branded personality has achieved a certain level of recognizability, future projects become easier to do. You don't have to constantly introduce yourself, re-explain projects, or beg for money. You've already established your credibility, therefore saving time to focus on the goal and get things done.

One great way to brand yourself and your cause is through the use of awards. While it may seem self-serving to apply for awards (which it can be if used for the wrong reasons), recognition from corporations and your peers can dramatically boost your efforts. You have credibility, so when you tackle a problem in your community, people and companies will want to pitch in and help, too.

A Good Deed

Movie stars have Oscars, stage actors have Tonys, and musicians have Grammys to recognize outstanding achievement. In the world of community service, there are also awards — big and small — and they, too, bring prestige, prominence, and credibility to community changers and their organizations. These awards can be the key to making an organization succeed beyond its wildest dreams.

In 1994, after returning from a weekend trip to Connecticut to accept the Albert Schweitzer Environmental Award, I realized that the benefits of being an award recipient went farther than the shiny plaque, $500 prize, and vegetarian lunch. The award could help me launch unique media campaigns about Earth 2000 and seek funding from corporations and wealthy philanthropists. The award gave me the stamp of approval needed to convince doubtful journalists and potential funders that Earth 2000 was a credible organization and not just a bunch of tree-hugging kids.

I also knew that Earth Day was just a month away — and that the lead time for seasonal/holiday articles for newspapers is also a month. It was a perfect opportunity to ask editors about profiling Earth 2000 for their Earth Day issues. I wrote what my friend Sharon, a public relations consultant, called "a tailored perfect news release" about having won the award. The title on the release read, "Local Teens Win International Environmental Award," with the emphasis being on "local" and "environmental."

I also wrote a personal letter to each journalist and editor receiving the release. It was a pitch letter, giving reason after reason why Earth 2000 was the only organization right for a feature and why their respective newspapers should give column inches to write about our organization.

A few days later, my hometown newspaper, the *Reading Eagle/Times*, contacted me about featuring Earth 2000 in their Lifestyle section. I was a bit surprised – not at their positive response but at their suggestion of putting our story in the Lifestyle section, next to sewing tips, Ann Landers, and wedding announcements. I wanted our story in the hard news section, next to stories about war-torn Bosnia and the president's new tax relief plan. But, following the simple public relations rule that "all publicity is good publicity," I accepted their offer.

The article helped to give Earth 2000 the needed credibility to get funds from a handful of corporations and philanthropists. And because the newspaper devoted two full pages to the article (an unusual decision, since most newspapers are usually pressed for space), it was hard to miss by the more than 100,000 Reading Eagle/Times subscribers. Many even sent checks to support Earth 2000. Today, I still use the article for personal public relations work.

Whether you use an award to gain media attention or to win the support of potential funders, you should remember to be innovative. An award is not just a prime photo opportunity, it is another way to help your group achieve its goals for a better world.

And the Winner is...

Awards, in general, range from local community awards that offer no financial incentive to competitive national awards with prizes as high as one million dollars. Here's an eclectic pick of a few national awards and their prizes (not necessarily awards for changing the world):

- Nobel Peace Prize $930,000
- Prudential Spirit of Community Award $5,000
- Make a Difference Day Award $10,000
  presented by actor Paul Newman
- Goldman Environmental Prize $75,000

Over the past few years, giving an award people who "do good" has become an increasingly prestigious trend. Do Something, a national organization founded by actor Andrew Shue, awarded $10,000 grants to ten people under the age of thirty who are working to improve their communities. On top of that, one winner received a $100,000 grand prize bonus. The 125 losing nominees didn't go away empty-handed: they each got a $500 consolation prize. With big-name sponsors like MTV, Mademoiselle, Blockbuster, Guess?, and America On-line, Do Something was able to distribute more than $200,000 in prizes for people who do good.

The annual event is supported by a lavish awards party, attended by top A-list celebrities, politicians, and philanthropists. With tables going for as high as $10,000 each, funds are raised to help support even more worthy projects. All of this in the name of doing good!

The Case For Rewarding Good Deeds

Many experts believe that reliance on external rewards destroys the intrinsic joy of volunteerism. Rewards may be useful for increasing productivity and creativity in the short term, but they can also decrease overall performance in the long run. Soon it becomes about winning, not about doing. This is only true, I believe, if the initial intention of the giver is to receive personal attention for their good deed. We often see pictures of CEOs giving away money to charity at lavish events; while this is great for the charity, you have to question how selfless the act really is.

Winning an award can boost the integrity and prominence of the organization you represent. Awards, when used properly and not for self-serving reasons, can help you get your foot in the door to see big funders, attract additional media attention to your cause, and add credibility to a new organization. When you win an award, you are basically receiving a stamp of approval: a group of strangers – the awards committee – is telling others that you're an effective, competent advocate for your organization.

In addition to the attention that the awards provide, many also offer financial prizes to winners as well as runner-ups. These range from $100 cash prizes to $100,000 grants to start a new community organization.

> *For ethical reasons, you should always donate the winnings to your organization or another non-profit group. Never, ever, keep the cash for yourself. Otherwise, you are setting yourself up for some harsh criticism and backlash from the community.*

There are awards for everyone – literally. In a few contests, especially the obscure ones, you are almost guaranteed to win. These receive so few eligible entries that virtually anyone who enters wins. In a few cases, there are more awards than applicants! I know these awards exist; I have won a few just because I was the *only one* who took the time to complete the application.

How Do I Find Out About Awards?

Unfortunately, there is no book that identifies awards given for community service. (Believe me I've looked through hundreds of books that had anything remotely to do with awards and prizes.) You've got to investigate and research a number of sources. Here are a few tips to finding out which awards are available.

Read the Newspaper Every Day

Check the Community Log, Area Highlights, Campus Notes, and any other section that posts notices of awards. If any award appeals to you, write or call for an application and rules form. College students should also read campus publications for listings.

Join Like-Minded National Organizations

Many national groups have awards programs honoring outstanding members. For example, the Humane Society of the United States (HSUS) has a program that offers monetary prizes to HSUS members who organize the most creative events for Farm Animals Awareness Week. Almost every national organization has at least one contest. Check the group's newsletter and other publications for notices.

Read Magazines

Be on the lookout for contests in mainstream and topic-oriented magazines. Often mainstream publications place tiny blurbs about national contests in their magazines. Topic-oriented publications usually list contests and award competitions that relate to their magazine.

Watch the Television News

Religiously watch the local televised nightly news shows to hear announcements of local awards. I discovered my local NBC affiliate organized the Jefferson Award, honoring local people who are "making their communities a better place to live."

Make Personal Contacts

Ask community leaders, sympathetic elected officials, and colleagues at national like-minded organizations to send you information about awards. Because they are usually the first people to receive information packets about current award opportunities in their respective fields, they can help you track down eligible award programs. I've won several awards just because a staff member at a national group took the time to send me an application.

A Few National Community-Service Awards

There are some good national programs that honor good works. Many of these organizations receive hundreds of applications every year for a very limited number of awards, so don't expect an easy win. But the process can be rewarding in other ways; as a judge for lots of these contests myself, I read hundreds of applications. I've often seen people walk away empty-handed, only for me to be so compelled by their application that I offer my services to help. You never know who is going to read your application.

Do Something

This organization awards grants to individuals under thirty years of age with creative community-building ideas. National grants are available through the New York office in the amount of $500; regional programs in Newark, New Jersey, Boston, and New York City offer local youth $500 grants and sponsor leadership courses.

Also, write for information about their BRICK award, an annual competition with a total of $250,000 in prize monies for community-based projects. Visit **www.dosomething.org**

Fund for Social Entrepreneurs (FFSE)

A project of Youth Service America, the FFSE contest seeks visionary leaders with bold and effective ideas for national and community-service ventures. Winners receive income stipends of $18,000 (year one) and $10,000 (year two), in addition to a $4,000 seed grant. Contact: **Youth Service America, 1101 15th Street, NW, Suite 200, Washington, DC 20005**; or call **(202) 296•2992**, or go on-line to **www.ysa.org**

Giraffe Project

America needs people with vision and courage — willing to stick their necks out and take responsibility for solving tough problems, from violence to hunger to pollution. The Giraffe Project has been finding these "giraffes" since 1982, and telling their stories in the media, from podiums, and in schools, inspiring others to stick their necks out, too. Visit **www.giraffe.org**

The Ingredients Of A Good Nomination Kit

To be noticed in the flood of award applications, you have to stand out. Creating a good nomination kit is like creating a good press kit. Read that again. Instead of sending a nomination kit with dozens of attachments (fifty news clippings, twenty-five letters of

> **Follow this rule at all times:**
> **Quality beats quantity.**

recommendation, etc.), send only the best material; the judges don't have time to weed out all of the unimportant papers. If you send a good-size nomination kit, you might even receive bonus points from the judges. Trust me: Quality over quantity.

Here's what a good nomination kit should include. Remember, every award is different and has its own special requirements. Be sure to tailor your kit. If you apply for several awards at the same time, you'll have an even better chance of winning. Keep trying and never, ever, give up!

Secrets of a Successful Application for an Award

- **COVER LETTER.** Type a one-page cover letter that has your name, address, and phone number at the top of the page. Concise letters are best. In the first paragraph, thank them for taking the time to consider your application. (You'd be surprised how many people forget.) Briefly discuss your project and credentials. Conclude with a sentence inviting them to contact you "at their convenience" with any questions.

- **APPLICATION FORM.** Be sure to fill out the application completely. If you don't, you risk being disqualified. If you're not sure how to answer a question, don't leave it blank! Call or write the award contact person and ask.

- **LETTERS OF RECOMMENDATION.** Ask community leaders, elected officials, and non-profit staffers to write letters of recommendation supporting your application. Be sure to get letters that aren't specifically written for a particular award. In other words, the letter should be addressed "To Whom It May Concern." Such generic letters of recommendation can be photocopied and used for other applications.

- **NEWS CLIPPINGS**. Send no more than three news clippings about your work. If possible, send actual copies of the newspaper or magazine. Be sure to mark the article.

- **BLACK-AND-WHITE PHOTOGRAPH**. Include a black-and-white headshot of yourself. When judges can relate a person's work to a face, it makes it more personable. These photos are more professional than color and the standard for many award competitions. Very few applicants remember to send a photo.

- **WRITING SKILLS**. If your writing skills aren't up to par, ask someone for help. And by all means, make sure all spelling is accurate. Write your application and have a friend edit it.

- **SUBMIT YOUR APPLICATION ON TIME**. Your application won't count if it doesn't make the deadline. Avoid using Federal Express or any other overnight mail service unless your nomination absolutely must arrive the very next day. In my experience, judges often read nominations as they come in. The applications that come in early get more attention because there are fewer of them. Don't have your application be part of the "flood" that comes in the day before the deadline.

- **USE RECYCLED PAPER**. Textured papers look nice and give you a "green" edge — bonus points for being ecologically aware. Don't use colored paper: it's difficult to copy from and makes your application look chintzy.

- **DON'T SEND ANYTHING SOILED OR EVEN SLIGHTLY DIRTY**. It seems obvious, but I've seen many otherwise brilliant applicants not win because the papers were stained with coffee or tea. One person even sent a nomination with dried blood on it. Gross!

What To Do After Winning

Sadly, many people don't take advantage of the benefits of being given an award for their efforts as a change agent. When managed well, the publicity from the award can bring benefits to your organization for several years, help to establish credibility and focus attention on your cause.

> *Do not send anything larger than a 5 x 7 photo.*
> *Big photos are overpowering and weaken the overall strength of your application.*

> *CAUTION!*
> *Be sure to get permission from the award organizers prior to sending anything out.*

Two Weeks Before an Awards Ceremony

- **SEND OUT A NEWS RELEASE**. Fax, mail, or e-mail a news release to every journalist in your immediate area announcing your win. If the ceremony is out of town, fax a news release to journalists in that town, too. In the release, invite them to cover the awards ceremony, to contact you for interviews, and to create a special feature article about your cause. If you get any coverage, try to get an address printed at the end of the article so interested readers can send donations or questions.

- **INVITE POTENTIAL FUNDERS TO THE CEREMONY**. Mail invitations to corporations and other potential funders you've been courting for grants. They may jump onto the praise bandwagon and give you a check at the ceremony as a show of support. It's good public relations for them, too.

- **SEND A THANK-YOU LETTER TO THE AWARDS COMMITTEE**. Avoid the temptation to save time by using e-mail to express your gratitude. There's something more meaningful about a handwritten note that will really get your point across.

What to Do After the Awards Ceremony

- **COLLECT NEWS CLIPPINGS**. Make photocopies of news clippings about the award. Keep them handy for future awards, grant proposals, and funding appeals. Whenever you write to someone important — like a senator or CEO — include a copy of the article. It'll add some credibility to your name and ensure a faster response.

- **THANK EVERYONE**. Send thank-you letters to anyone who helped you win the award. Thank the English teacher who edited your application, members from your group, people you met at the ceremony, journalists who wrote about you, and anyone else who either helped you on the application or showed up to attend the ceremony.

Recycle The Award Into An Introduction

Ever notice how people introduced as Nobel Laureates receive more attention than plain, old Bob Smith gets? At a grassroots level, the award may be enough to convince local schools and Rotary clubs to invite you to present a speech. In their eyes, it's prestigious to have an award-winning change agent as a guest speaker — which means more willing ears for your cause. Sometimes you may even receive an honorarium for your services as a speaker. This is a payment for your time and trouble.

If your topic is unique enough, you might want to consider getting representation from a speakers' bureau to book your talks at colleges, conferences, and corporate retreats. Some good agencies to contact:

- The American Program Bureau. The "world's largest speakers bureau" represents world leaders such as Bishop Desmond Tutu and Mikhail Gorbachev and youth-oriented speakers like former cast members of MTV's "The Real World" and CBS' "Survivor." Check them out at **www.apbspeakers.com**

- Lordly and Dame represents speakers ranging from luminary Maya Angelou to rocker Henry Rollins. Visit **www.lordly.com** to learn more.

- Greater Talent Network. This agency focuses more on speakers fit for the corporate world: the founder's of Ben & Jerry's ice cream, net expert Aliza Sherman, and CEOs of new media companies like I-village and flooz. Visit **www.greatertalent.com**

It's tough to get represented by these agencies. If you'd like to talk at schools and special events, you can often book yourself. Send some info about your work to the special events or lecture bureau office at higher education institutions. Their job is to bring in unusual and relevant speakers for their student body to meet and hear.

Create Your Own Award

If you discover there is a need for an award, start one. You don't need a lot of money, just some time and good marketing skills. Use the skills you have learned from attending award ceremonies to create your own ideal award. Spread the word through the media to find prospective recipients. By developing your own award program, you not only honor those working on your issue, but you also bring additional media attention to the overall cause.

Awards are a powerful tool in furthering your cause and organization. But don't fall into the "glory trap" by letting awards dominate your life. When you win an award, you serve as an example to others to become active members of the community; it won't work is you come across as a pretentious, conceited snob. Use awards to advance your cause, not yourself.

If You Liked This Chapter, You'll Love:

- Apply for the Hometown Canada Community Service Award. If you've donated some time, money, or resources to your community, you can apply for either a bronze, silver, or gold award. Learn more at **www.hometown canada.com/serviceaward**

- In the United States, the Hometown United States Community Service Award is available at **www.home townusa.com/serviceaward**.

- If you don't have access to a printer or a place that can print out color documents for you, do it on-line. At **Kinkos.com**, you can upload your document on their website, choose color or black and white printing (including paper type, binding options, and more), and order next day business delivery via Federal Express.

- If you're looking for a project, the Planning Guide for *USA Weekend*'s Make A Difference Day is an excellent place to start. They have sections on how employers, teens, college students, and families can make a difference. Visit their website at **www.usaweekend.com** to get started.

- Take pictures of all the good work you're doing without spending a lot of your budget. At **www.snapfish.com**, you pay only for the shipping and handling: the online sponsors pay the rest. You can even view your photos on-line at their website for re-ordering.

10

internships:

Finding a Wealth of Knowledge in Your Own Backyard

"You live and learn.
At any rate, you live."

Douglas Adams

IF you've ever tried to learn something new — like a second language, a sport, or a craft — you know it's nearly impossible to master it in just a day, let alone by reading a book. But you also know that to be good at something new, you start with a first step. You took the first step in learning how to make a difference by picking up this book, and for that, you must be commended. But to further your education — learning new ways to be the difference, in particular — you must open your eyes and ears and allow yourself to absorb all the world has to offer. The world, as the saying goes, is your classroom.

If you're a young person in high school, a recent college graduate, or even a retiree, an internship is a good place to get first hand experience. Unlike a paid job, an internship is easy to obtain, has flexible hours, and offers truly diversified skills that you'll pick up from the time you spend at an organization. First, Internship 101.

What Is An Internship?

The verb "to intern" means "to shut up closely so that escape is impossible or unlikely." Frightening. But despite the definition, an internship is not a prison sentence. It is a volunteer job: an organization "hires" you to do work usually done by paid employees. Many companies and non-profits bring in interns for one simple reason: they can't afford to employ additional staff. In most cases, you are not paid a penny for your work. So why work full time for zero pay? Simple: experience and connections. In the entertainment industry, the tradition is well-established: highly-educated graduates work as interns or in the mail room of big-name talent agencies. There, they learn new skills, gain the trust of upper management, and eventually work their way up to becoming an agent.

An internship with your favorite national organization can turn into a full-time position. According to a recent study by Northwestern University, 58% of interns are eventually offered jobs with their host employers. Fifty-eight percent! Because corporations and non-profits receive stacks of resumes for a few job openings, they are more likely to hire someone they already know – such as someone who has been an intern with them. It is worth the investment of working for three months without pay for the opportunity to receive a salaried position in the organization of your choice.

When I was seventeen years old, I accepted a summer internship at a wildlife protection organization in Washington, DC. The three-month experience wasn't something I could profit from financially, but I knew it would be a gold mine of contacts and experience. I had no idea at the time how real-world involvement with staff meetings, lobbying, and writing could help me in the future, but I did know it was an important step for me to take.

Granted, lots of my time was spent fetching lunches for staff, opening mail, answering phones, and making photocopies. At times, it felt I was a work-for-free assistant. In fact, I didn't even have a desk there; I set-up a card table in the corner of the conference room and pretended it was my own private workspace.

But I did learn things that I couldn't pick up from any book or lecture. I was observing strategists, lobbyists, public relations experts, and others working together – plotting campaigns and using minimal resources to have maximum impact. It's tough to articulate in words, but when you see people in action, you pick up ideas, skills, and nuances that really affect you in a positive way.

I can't entirely credit my three-months there for making me the person who I am today; there are so many individuals, moments of dumb luck, and personal perseverance that have been crucial to my development. But I also can't deny what the internship provided – getting me started on my path in life.

What Can I Expect From An Internship?

Every internship is different. If you intern with an organization that mainly lobbies elected officials, you may be expected to coordinate meetings with political staffers and send position papers to senators. If you intern with a non-profit publication, you may be expected to interview people for articles and spell-check copy for upcoming issues. But every intern should expect to do clerical work – like photocopying and filing – at least 25 to 30 percent of the time.

To help you understand the various internships that non-profit organizations offer, here's a selection from a few U.S. national ones, including the duties, housing availability, pay (if any), and application requirements. Notice the diversity of each internship program.

Center for Science in the Public Interest

Interns work in the Washington, DC, office on nutrition science policy and/or food safety issues. Internships last ten weeks with a minimum wage for undergraduate students. Application process: send cover letter, resume, writing sample, two letters of recommendation, and official transcript of courses and grades. **www.cspinet.org**

Children's Defence Fund

Interns provide important staff support by conducting surveys, drafting reports, developing databases, attending congressional hearings, and providing logistical support for workshops and conferences. Interns are not paid and housing is not provided. There are eleven divisions for specialized internships, including the media department and the office of government affairs. Application process: send application, cover letter (which serves as a writing sample), a resume, and three references. **www.childrens defense.org**

Fellowship of Reconciliation

Interns work in three departments for this national peace and justice organization. Duties include racial and economic justice program coordination, communications, media relations, and local group organizing. Interns receive free housing, medical insurance, and a $600-a-month stipend. Application process: send for an application. **www.forusa.org**

Locating Internships

First and foremost, you must find out about current internship opportunities. Locating the dream internship is like researching which college or university is right for you. Research everything, then reject what doesn't suit.

• Sit down and make a list of every national organization you would enjoy working for. Then cut the list to six. Call the personnel director of each and ask for information about internship opportunities and an application form.

• Ask contacts at other organizations for information. Staff at those organizations without an internship program can help you locate good ones. They can also warn you about dead-end internships they might have personally experienced. Learn from their mistakes.

• Pick up a current copy of a publication produced by an organization in your field of choice. Check out the classified section for the latest internships being offered by like-minded organizations. Some internships will offer financial incentives in their ads to attract prospective applicants. A list of some of these publications can be found at the end of this chapter.

• After receiving some detailed information about internships, discard those that don't interest you. Chances are you'll be unhappy at those places. Also, set aside internships that do not fit within your time frame. For example, if you planned on interning for only one month and a group requires a minimum three-month stay, file that application for future reference.

> *If an organization doesn't have an internship program, offer your services anyway. Some groups are so busy and overworked that such a program has not been launched. You could be the answer to their heavy workload and, in the long run, have a better chance of future employment with the organization.*

The Application Process

An internship is just like any other job. All you need to do is to apply for the position. But in most cases, your application is the only way the personnel director can get a sense of your personality and qualifications. There is no room for modesty or mistakes in your application. Here are a few tips to make it extraordinary.

Before You Even Start

Make photocopies of the application before you begin to fill it in. People mess up on their applications, so it's a good idea to have extra copies just in case. Also, be sure to use a pen when filling out an application.

Include a Resumé

A resumé (a summary of your qualifications and experience) gives the personnel director a quick look at your education, work experience, and special skills. Internship resumés should also include any successful projects you have conceived and completed. Also include any awards you may have received. Even high school students should put together a resumé or, at the least, a list of qualifications. Writing a good resumé takes a lot of practice. Look for books on resumé writing at your local library or check out *How You Really Get Hired* by John L. LaFevre (New York: Prentice Hall, 1992). You can also get lots of tips and templates at **www.free-resume-tips.com**

Be Thorough

Be sure to fill out the entire application completely. If something doesn't apply to you, write "N/A" to indicate not applicable. Good grammar and punctuation are crucial. And always, *always* check spelling.

Answer Tricky Questions Intelligently

For example, if they ask "What is your worst quality?" reply with a positive quality. "My worst quality is my overeagerness to get a project done as quickly as possible. I just can't relax." A wrong answer would be: "I'm lazy."

Include a Photograph of Yourself

You make a more personal impression on the personnel director if you include a photograph. You don't need a professional photo; a Polaroid will do. Just remember to keep the photo smaller than five by seven inches.

Include News Clippings and Letters of Recommendation

Send photocopies of the best news clippings and letters of recommendations you have. Doing so will prove your competence and ability to get the job done.

Be a Neat Freak

Divide your materials into sections (e.g., news clippings, essay, letters of recommendation) and put them into a new folder. Use clean, unwrinkled paper. Neatness counts big-time.

Don't Lie

False information will come back to haunt you sooner or later. Start your internship with a clean slate. Don't lie.

You can also learn valuable lessons by interning with a corporation. If you intern at a public relations firm, you'll learn the nuts and bolts of the news media industry. If you work for a new media company, you'll learn how websites work, what builds them, and what runs them. All of these skills can help you in bigger ways than you initially think.

Negotiate Your Internship

Contrary to popular belief, it is okay to negotiate the terms of your internship after landing one. Non-profit groups depend heavily on interns to keep their organizations afloat, so you can make some reasonable demands if you decide to accept their internship offer. Before you say yes to any internship, decide what you want to get out of it and ask for it from the start. Here's what you can probably get with enough persistence:

Money

Even if they specifically state they do not pay their interns, ask the organization to provide a living stipend for transportation, food, and other living expenses. Start high, around $1,000 a month, and negotiate your way down. But remember, even if you only get $100 a month, that's still better than nothing — most interns receive zero compensation.

Housing

If you need a place to live during your internship, and they say they'll provide housing, make sure you have that commitment in writing before you move.

A Written Learning Agreement

Ask for a "learning agreement." This is a written contract that outlines what an intern is expected to do and what work experience the intern will receive in return. You will not only impress the personnel director by being so knowledgeable, but you will also protect yourself from getting a dud internship.

Regular Meetings

Ask to have a weekly meeting with the executive director or your supervisor to discuss your progress. Doing so will help keep the lines of communication open. These are good opportunities to pitch new project ideas, introduce innovative ways to streamline the office, and do anything else to impress the head honcho.

If you sense your employer is getting disturbed by any of your demands, let them go. But don't accept anything you feel is totally unfair. The best way to create a fair contract is to have both parties willing to compromise.

Free Weekends

Many interns are expected to be available at a moment's notice. This is not fair to you. Have your learning agreement state that you will not work on weekends; you deserve to have some time to yourself! Try to get an agreement that states you are not obliged to work more than forty hours a week.

Reaping The Intern Benefits

When everything falls into place, your internship can lead to a great career in your field of interest. Many people who started off as interns are now high-level staff members or even presidents of organizations. But to make sure you do everything right in your transition to an actual salary, follow these tips:

Keep a Journal

From Day 1 to Day 100 of your internship, keep a log of everything you did. "On August 13, I created an action alert to notify our 50,000 members about a new White House plan to discontinue funding for Head Start." You can use your accomplishments to strengthen your case for full-time employment with either your host employer or other organizations.

Notify Your Supervisors

Three weeks before the end of your internship, notify your supervisor that you will be searching for a salaried position in your field. Ask that they consider you for any current or future employment opportunities. If they have no jobs, ask them to recommend you to other like-minded organizations.

Think Of It As A Test.

When interning, remember to think of this opportunity as a test of your intelligence, competence, and creativity. Be part of the inventive process at work and become a team player. If, at the end of your internship, your co-workers realize that your absence will have an adverse effect on their work, you may have just landed yourself a job.

Ask for an Evaluation

A week before leaving your internship, ask your supervisors for an evaluation of your work. Their comments, if positive, will be crucial in finding employment with other organizations.

Send a Thank-You Note

Thank everyone for the opportunity to work with them. Your courtesy will keep your work fresh in everyone's mind. Also, your attention to detail will increase the possibility of a career at that organization.

But I Don't Want A Job

Not all interns want to land a full-time job. Many people intern with their favorite organization just for the experience and fun of it: they are excited about working full-time with their favorite group, helping out at the national level. Some people even spend their entire summer vacation interning in an organization's office as a way of making a contribution. They see it as a rewarding experience and love every minute they're there. Here are some other benefits:

Resumé

Adding your internship experience to a resumé can improve future employment chances with any type of business (profit and non-profit). Employers like to see individuals with diverse experience as well as strong educational and personal skills.

Improved Skills

You can use your skills to create or to improve your own grassroots organization. The ideas and strategies you'll pick up from just one week of interning will be invaluable for future campaign efforts.

Contacts

It's easier to contact people at national groups about your own projects after your internship. Because they know you, staffers will be more willing to help you. Friends are more likely to help friends.

> *Interning can lead to a successful career with a non-profit organization. You won't get rich working for a non-profit, but you can reap other benefits: knowing you're working full-time to ease the exploitation, the agony, and the misery humans and animals face in our world. It will enrich your soul.*

For the Fun of It

Interning can be an enjoyable and fulfilling experience. From building houses in a Costa Rican rain-forest to lobbying legislators in Wisconsin, internships are great opportunities to make a real difference while having a lot of fun.

If You Liked This Chapter, You'll Love:

Almost every major national non-profit organization maintains a website. Check out their sites for listings on internship and job availability. And don't be afraid to call them directly and ask, too.

Some good job listing sites, like **www.hotjobs.com** and **www.monster.com**, also list internships. What's beneficial about these sites is that the information is constantly updated. It's a good idea to visit these sites daily to keep abreast of the latest opportunities that are available in your community.

Here are some guidebooks on locating internships with your favorite organization:

- The Environmental Careers Organization (ECO) lists environmental internships. Write: **286 Congress Street, 3rd Floor, Boston, MA 02110**, or call **(617) -426•4375**.

- America's Promise pulls together the talents and resources of companies, public service groups, and children's service providers in the United States, in order to strengthen kids' minds, bodies, and character as well. They have lots of ideas about how you can help. Go on-line at **www.americaspromise.org**

- Also check out the Princeton Review's annual listing of internships available in the United States. *America's Top Internships* and *The Internship Bible* (New York: Random House) are the best directories available: they list internship opportunities with groups ranging from Greenpeace to Amnesty International. All information is updated quarterly.

- In Canada, Youth Internship Canada (YIC) provides funding to employers who create "meaningful work experiences for unemployed and underemployed youth." The goal is to give young people valuable work experience that they can apply in the future. Canadian companies seeking funding and young people wanting to get involved can learn more at **www.youth.hrdc-drhc.gc.ca**

- The Corporation of National Service works to combat challenges such as illiteracy, poverty, crime, and environmental problems by working with governor-appointed state commissions, non-profits, faith-based groups, schools, and other civic organizations. The three major initiatives are AmeriCorps, Learn and Serve

America, and the National Senior Service Corps. If you're interested in giving more of your time to a national service project, this is a great place to start. Go on-line to **www.cns.gov**.

an afterword

SINCE the publication of *Generation React,* several years have passed and people often ask what I'm doing today

When I was eighteen years old, I retired as CEO of Earth 2000 National to focus on new goals and aspirations. I felt the goals I achieved as a teenage advocate were important: they showed that young people could actually have a powerful voice in the environmental movement. Our campaigns were successful and I know we inspired thousands of idealistic young people and helped some of them to become leading public advocates.

Today, I am the president of Danny Seo Media Ventures, Inc., a cause-related lifestyle company producing books, television programming, Internet content, and even merchandise related to the idea that you can marry concern for the planet with style. With a team of the brightest leaders in the entertainment industry, we're working to bring our message to the biggest audience possible.

My feeling is that those of us in the environmental movement tend to "preach to the choir." I want to reach out to people who rarely hear information about the environment – to give them ways to volunteer and to make a difference. I believe that by lecturing at colleges and by creating an interactive lifestyle television program which first – and foremost – entertains and also educates, the environmental message will really get to the mainstream.

I couldn't help but notice that the environmental movement has become stale: very few people celebrate Earth Day any more. I decided to re-evaluate my efforts in order to help re-energize the movement. I was tired of being labeled a granola cruncher with no fashion sense. I knew many other concerned people who didn't deserve to be stereotyped that way, either. I have always felt that you can marry style with concern for the planet — and that's exactly what I've set out to do.

I believe that to convince people to truly change their ways, you can't use force or tell them what to do. Instead, I make eco-friendly living a lifestyle choice, providing information to show how wonderful — even luxurious — vegetarian food, all-natural materials, and even recycled products can be. At my company, we emphasize style and simplicity first, making it our top priority in everything we do. If a 100% organic cotton sheet is too expensive or the quality of cotton is poor, we won't use it. But we will do everything possible to ensure that our sheets contain the highest possible percentage of good-quality organic cotton.

My company is growing at a tremendous rate and we're planning many exciting projects. But as we grow into a successful for-profit venture, I believe we can still do the right thing: share the fruits of labor and remember our roots. That's why I continue to devote a large percentage — a minimum of fifteen percent — of our proceeds to charitable causes, including the environment, children, and housing for people in need. In addition to giving funds, I continue to share our simple ideas — which I have called "fast philanthropy" — to encourage novice change agents to give a few minutes each day to make a difference. Since the Internet has increased the speed of living, it's important to show people how they can use it to do something quick and easy to help someone in need or to improve the community — in just a few minutes.

When I was twelve years old, I told my friends we were going to save the planet by the year 2000. Now that the millennium has passed, I realize that we still have a long way to go. But I am energized by a new sense of purpose in my life: I want to see how compassion and commerce can be brought together. Growing up, I believed the only way to really change the world was to do it for purely altruistic motives. But now I've changed my view: business has to do the right thing, too. And as an individual who has had the benefit of being both a non-profit leader and a business executive, I believe our company can do good business *and* make a difference. Using the power of the Internet, television, books, and our environmentally-responsible product line to effect real-world solutions, our company is truly on the forefront of a new environmental movement.

Entertainment, merchandising, and environmentalism may seem like an odd combination. But to really change how people live, you have to make it easy to implement change. I believe as a company we can not only create a good product, but do a good job at making a difference, too. It's a rarely used business model, granted, but given the importance of changing the world, we hope to provide a way people can participate in that change through the choices they make about seemingly insignificant things. And collectively, whether it's by buying an organic cotton towel or practicing a "fast philanthropy" technique, we'll have power in numbers.

Write to me and share your ideas and thoughts.

Danny Seo

c/o Danny Seo Media Ventures
Dept. BD
302A West 12th Street, Suite 177
New York, NY 10014

www.dannyseo.com